Mrs Josie
864 T
Jewish Hosp.

You Deserve To Be Happy

You Owe It To Yourself

Ruth Ann Polston

D0110783

Harvest House Publishers
Irvine, California 92714

Unless otherwise noted, Scriptures are quoted from THE LIVING BIBLE ©
Tyndale House Publishers 1971, 1974 and are used by permission.

Scripture quotations from the **Revised Standard Version**, copyrighted 1946, 1952
1971, 1973 and are used by permission.

Scripture quotations from the **New American Standard Bible**, © The Lockman
Foundation 1960, 1962, 1963, 1968, 1971, 1972, 1973, 1975 and are used by
permission.

YOU DESERVE TO BE HAPPY

Copyright © 1978 Harvest House Publishers
Irvine, California 92714

Library of Congress Catalog Card Number: 77-94045
ISBN #0-89081-126-1

Printed in the United States of America

CONTENTS

III. YOUR PROBLEMS

Part I

Your Home

Part I

1. THE YEAR OF THE WOMAN

Something new is always being broadcast across the world. The world is changing fast. As soon as an idea is born, it's on its way to history. It would appear that women never had it so good. Many drive their own car, work out of the home, eat out almost every day, and get baby-sitters for almost every occasion.

While the woman seeks freedom, she is in jeopardy of losing it.

I have empathy for single Christian girls. We have noted that many boys have uncertainties as the time of the wedding approaches. They feel insecure. They're not sure they can cope with the responsibility of two people. It's not unusual to see a wedding date scratched from our calendar because the boy was unsure of marital responsibility.

A Christian man shared his painful experience with his daughter and boyfriend. The couple lived together openly and experimented with various drugs. Any time the father shared a spiritual experience with her, the daughter would claim she'd felt the same on drug trips. Something truly demonic had entered their home. Her dad seemed powerless to change the situation, but he and his wife continued to pray.

One day he heard uncontrolled sobs coming from his daughter's bedroom. When he approached her, he saw her sprawled figure, beating the bed in anguish. He discovered that his daughter's world had crumbled. Her boyfriend had walked out of her life after taking from her the precious, sacred things which she could have brought to the marriage altar. He gathered her in his arms and began to pray. As he prayed, her agony turned to prayers of repentance. She soon was immersed in the love of Christ and her wounded life began to heal.

What is the role of the woman? Where is "freedom" taking us? The best thing a woman has ever had going for her is marriage. The freedom she lunges for outside of marriage eludes her.

A married woman finds herself when she loses her independent self in her man. The greatest motivator of a man is a woman who thinks her husband is great, and isn't afraid to tell him so. Anyone can be won through approval. A man needs one person—above all others—who thinks he's the greatest; his wife. The wise woman will build his ego. In losing her independent self, she can usually make a prince out of an ordinary thinking man. The power a woman has over a man is awesome and frightening. Few men have succeeded in spite of an unworthy wife.

John Wesley was probably one of the exceptions. His wife did everything possible to destroy him. She accused him in public, railed on him in private gatherings, and physically assaulted him at home. Perhaps this is the secret of his many books, written on horseback as he visited his churches. When my husband and I were conducting a tour in London, we visited Wesley's home, prayer chamber and the room from which he died. I read the list of noble men of his time who were around his bedside as he died, and noted that Mrs. Wesley was not among them.

Few men scale the scorn of a woman. A wife can kill her husband's happiness when he opens the front door by a shrug, indifference, a dirty house, a dull appearance or pure neglect.

My husband and I once prayed with a lady versed in spiritual matters but experiencing deep depression. Trying to arrive at the root of her problem, we asked her to follow us in a prayer. We first confessed allegiance to Jesus Christ as the Lord of her life. Then we prayed a prayer of submission concerning her husband's headship of their home. She refused to repeat it. She parroted that she would submit only to Jesus Christ. Her confusion increased, and she is now more depressed than ever. Her family is alienated from her and her sanity is questioned.

"For rebellion is as bad as the sin of witchcraft . . ." (1 Sam. 15:23) Without realizing it, this woman can no longer discern right and wrong. She failed to take the whole counsel of God, and lost her way spiritually and emotionally.

The Bible does not give assurance that doing right will produce ideal circumstances in our home. Some things may never change. But we can change. We may have the blessing of knowing we are in God's will. If life hands us a bitter cup, it can sweeten in the drinking. The thorn may be an instrument to glory in. If so, His strength shall be made perfect in weakness. We can win the battle but lose the war.

It's the year of the woman. Only we can decide what kind of woman. If the husband rises, the wife rises with

him. If he falls, she falls with him. Make this the best
year of the woman.

2.   I THOUGHT I HAD A PERFECT MARRIAGE

"Where did I go wrong? What's the matter with me? I
thought this could never happen to us."

This is a sad echo heard from too many victims of
troubled marriages. Certainly couples must be naive to
conclude a marriage just erupts without some fore-
warning signs. Evidently the biggest answer to such a
pathetic situation is lack of communication.

It seems that it is possible for marriage partners
to—live together, going through all the routine marital
responsibilities—after having the fire of love and
commitment go out.

"I thought we had the perfect marriage," the
disillusioned husband stated. He appeared to be kind,
sympathetic, and to possess all the traits a Christian
husband should have. However, he lacked one
ingredient: He failed to take leadership to make strong
decisions. Rather than to speak up and let their
dissatisfaction show, each marriage partner had
maintained a quiet passivity about one another's lack.

Dont mistakenly conclude that passivity is an
indication of a perfect marriage. Buried aggravations
can erupt too late. It is better to keep communications
open. Tell the other mate, frankly, what you like or
dislike. Many emotions are smothered in a pillow at
night. We need to develop an honest, open relationship
with our spouse. Beware when you feel you never know
what your mate is thinking.

Be aware of the telltale signs of a growing marital

break. How do you rate yourself when it comes to fulfilling your role as a marriage partner? Perhaps reviewing your "position" in regard to the following points of discussion will aid you in evaluating the status of your marital bliss, and how much effort you really are exerting in keeping the communication channels open between you and your mate.

1. *Role-playing.* We can play the part of something without being the part. Don't be afraid to let the other person know you have feelings. It develops a healthy dependence on the other person. Better be open around your mate than someone outside your home.

2. *Be natural.* Men are big boys more than women are big girls. A man needs to let the "big boy" in him show sometimes, and the wife should allow it. A man needs variety. Women shouldn't challenge his ball game, his hunting expedition, his pursuit of variety. Be interested in all he does and, as much as possible, be a part of it.

3. *Don't be under bondage to each other.* Husbands and wives should be able to relate on everything. If you can't talk about religion, learn to talk in a way that doesn't put the other person in an inferior position. When we consciously or unconsciously cause another person to feel inferior around us, they will sooner or later excuse themselves from our company. A person who shuts himself off behind an invisible wall can be tuning out that which threatens his self-image. We are under a divine trust to bring out the best in our mates. This can only be done by approval. Lack of approval is killing and can easily be found elsewhere. No one should have to go out of their home to find approval.

4. *Preoccupation with children.* No matter how demanding our parental responsibilities may be, our mates are #1. A neglected mate may soon not be a mate. Keep your priorities in good standing. A pleasant relationship between Mom and Dad is more healthy to a child's well being than over-protection of the child. Children of divorced or arguing parents have far more psychological problems than a child who comes first—*after* Mom and Dad.

5. *Keep contemporary in your appearance.* Neither mate marries a slovenly person and doesn't deserve one after marriage. Whatever it took to keep you looking attractive and physically clean before you wed, will be just as necessary after marriage. Always be looking for little changes. Wear your hair differently. Buy a new scarf to accent a favorite dress. Be your best self early in the morning. Don't insult your mate by dressing like you don't care.

6. *Keep creating in your home.* Always keep a project of improvement going in your home. Anything that makes for variety, change, and interest is pleasant to come home to. Change your furniture around. Put the pictures on another wall. Paint some furniture.

7. *Keep an enthusiastic, vivacious spirit.* Talk about happy, wholesome things. Practice speaking positively about everything and everybody.

8. *Always seek to make your mate feel special.* A little note in the sandwich, an unexpected hug, a date, a sudden trip to the corner for an ice cream cone adds luster to your romance. Let no one be more attentive or complimentary than you. Instead of saying, "Your suit looks good on you," say, "You make your suit look good!"

9. *Keep goals.* Write goals for your lives together as well as writing down individual goals. Review, renew, and rewrite your goals often so you avoid stagnation in accomplishments. You develop partnership toward something worthwhile. Plan well in advance for a big trip together.

The Bible says, "He (God) gives families to the lonely . . ." (Psa. 68:6). You need no strong attachments outside of your family. The Bible says to . . ."know we no man after the flesh" (2 Cor. 5:16, KJV) The only safe and permanent way to know people is "after the spirit."

Counseling sessions involving couples who are no longer able to adequately communicate with one another, often reveal that one of the marriage partners has developed a close friendship outside of the family unit. No matter how innocent it may seem, it is unwise. Beware of the best friend, the neighbor who "neighbors" too frequently, or the person who complains about the inadequacy of their mate to fill their need. The common lament is, "I thought it could never happen to us."

Because a home is Christian doesn't mean it is altogether safe. The presumptuous relationships of Christians have sown many a destructive seed. In Nehemiah's day each man stood on his wall to protect his own family from the enemy. The enemy still seeks to get over your wall, into your family unit, and to make havoc. Guard your home. Guard your affection. Guard your friendships. The thief is at the door and has come "to steal, kill and destroy."

Plan, pray and work toward coming down to life's end with destiny fulfilled, lives untarnished and no regrets.

Wives, submit to your own husbands *as* to the Lord.
Husbands, love your wives as Christ loved the
church (see Eph. 5:22, 25).

You can't improve on it. It's the perfect formula for
the nearest-to-perfect marriage.

3. LEARN TO HARMONIZE

It is possible for God to work where harmony does
not exist, but it's not probable. All of God's works,
from the beginning until now, are based on harmony.
Nature demands harmony. All of nature cooperates to
bring about order; and from this order there is beauty.

We have a variety of flowers in our backyard which
come up every year. It's interesting to note that the
tulips and the forget-me-nots don't spring up at the same
time. The lilies blossom and leave their aroma for a few
days and then the peonies take their turn.And so it goes,
throughout the summer. One flower lives, serves and
gives way to the next. Some proudly blossom all
summer long, but others serve their purpose and give
way. Nature doesn't compete.

The blackbirds usually try to champion the yard, but
the tricky sparrows, wrens, robins and blue jays hold
their own; and none ever goes hungry. The squirrels
respect the rabbits. They prefer the nuts to lettuce
anyway.

Beasts of prey play an important part in the balance
of nature. Even in dying, one species gives life to
another. Salmon fight their way upstream every year,
for thousands of miles, to spawn and die to give life to
others.

Perfect harmony in life always requires its balance of dying. The Bible plainly tells us that our outward man perishes every day. Even this process is necessary to emancipate the inner man from his prison.

But beyond the body a part of us should be dying every day. Jesus said, "Greater love has no man than this, that a man lay down his life for his friends" (John 15:13, *RSV*).

How do we lay down our life? Certainly Jesus did not mean all of us would be offered up on a wooden cross to save a soul. The apostle Paul said, "I die daily" (1 Cor. 15:31, *NASB*). How does this dying take place? By living positively in a negative world. No one said it would be easy. But without positive faith and actions, there is no harmony. Jesus did not say we could live peaceably with all men. But Paul says, "if it be possible, live peaceably with all men" (Rom. 12:18, *KJV*).

Harmony in human relations is when I allow "he to be he, and me to be me." How many human relationships could be healed if we would practice this kind of harmony? Keeping peace at the price of principle brings no peace because it has no truth to back it up. Most of our lack of harmony results because we have *made* something our business which is really none of our business.

When we have a habit of creating waves wherever we go, it is an indication of a lack of harmony within ourselves. Jesus possessed inner harmony, yet who can deny His waves? The "waves" created by Jesus represented conclusions drawn by those who wanted to strip him to conformity. Those people who loved truth and earnestly sought truth were never in conflict with

Jesus. Our minds are so inconceivably tricky, that it's fairly easy to determine that the other man has to be all wrong and we have to be all right. A man who is totally correct doesn't usually have to prove it at the expense of injury to another. The person who is unteachable can fairly well conclude that his wisdom is not from above.

How then, can we live harmoniously in an unharmonious family or world? If we must always tread softly, so as not to ingender peace, we could be lost in the crowd; we'd end up our life with, "Here lies Jim Jones, who lived and died," written on our tombstone.

I'd like to share several "harmony" principles which must exist in order to achieve peace and progress:

1. Jesus said to come out from among them and be ye separate. If you insist on cultivating relationships with non-Christians in your world, you cannot keep your mind centered on what you have to do. Allow old worn-out relationships to cease if they are no longer good for you.

2. Keep a single mind about God's goal for your life and allow others the same privilege. If you are both in truth, you will eventually come out together, safe at last.

3. Allow some of you to "die" when you have opportunity to allow another person a right, which you think you deserve. If forfeiting that right doesn't mar your ultimate goals, you can grow spiritually, and in harmony with that other individual, by being flexible and yielding to their desires.

4. Jesus said, "Greet no one on the way" (Luke 10:4, *NASB*). A wise man said what is sacred should be kept secret. Joseph told his dream as soon as he received it

and it caused disharmony among his brothers. Later he was able to keep silent when his brothers appeared in Egypt and bowed before him.

5. Resist no evil. Sometimes evil is God's tool, a negative agent, to bring about His purpose. When we resist something, we give it power. If we make a practice of fighting everything evil or disagreeable, we soon find our mind has no place to contain pure and lovely thoughts. We are against something before we even know what it is. I'm reminded of the man who was unable to attend a business meeting. He took time to telephone the chairman to leave this message: "Whatever they will be discussing, I am against it!"

6. "Come to terms quickly with your opponent before it is too late" (Matt. 5:25). What if you get guilt on your conscience? What if we do something which is not in keeping with our true or Christian character? Don't whisk it under the rug. Agree quickly. Unless you speedily make it right, in you or with another, you will have to be delivered to your own conscience which will judge you. You will stay in a prison of your own making until you pay the uttermost farthing of repentance.

7. "Don't let the sun go down with you still angry—get over it quickly" (Eph. 4:26). Make no place in your mind for grudges to take root. Living free of negative emotions is a must for harmonious living.

You are a permanent part of life. Since you are here to stay, why not enjoy the journey and make it more enjoyable for yourself, for your family, and for others?

Learn to blend in with life and not fight it. Become a force which pushes life forward and doesn't obstruct the flow. Play your part in life's rhythm. Learn to harmonize.

4. BE WISE AND SAVE YOUR MARRIAGE

I don't often share the letters that I receive, but my friend has given special permission for her letter to be used. I believe the letter speaks for itself:

Dear Ruth Ann,

Praise the Lord for your message today! I have never heard of your program before over KWKY until this morning. As I listened I was blessed and learned from your teaching.

The Lord spoke to my heart about writing and sharing with you what He has done and is doing in my life and our marriage.

During two and a half years my husband and I were separated four different times and finally divorced in June of 1976. My husband and I were remarried in October of 1976. My husband and three children have all accepted Christ. The joy that fills our home is wonderful.

My husband was a hard man and my life was threatened many times. I once had a broken jaw; I lived in constant fear. All of my Bibles were burned. And to think, a heart so hard now sings and gives praises to God. He weeps when a gospel song is heard.

When my husband filed for divorce, I felt the Lord speaking to me and saying, "If you will give him to me for awhile I will give him back to you whole. Just trust me." We had been married 19 years. I said, "O.K. Lord, I will trust you."

Our situation was so different. The day we signed the divorce papers there was still love between us. We walked out of the court house hand in hand, and kissed before we parted. But now I realize why it had to be that way. When I got turned on to the Lord, I was going to push what I had received on my husband and make him want it—like it or not. I thought it was so great to have peace and to be free that I wanted him to have it like I did.

I was like a bear in a china closet. I destroyed everything I touched. At length, the Lord made me realize *I* was the rebellious one. I didn't want to come under the authority of my husband—I was going to do it my way. He knew my heart and His mercy turned me around when I opened my eyes and stopped putting the blame on my husband for his spiritual needs. I found it is not hard for a Christian woman to destroy her home when she goes her own way.

There is only one assurance we have for the victory in our homes and that is to follow God's order in His Word. The Lord made 1 Timothy 2:10,11 come alive. "And the women should be the same way, quiet and sensible in manner and clothing. Christian women should be noticed for being kind and good, not for the way they fix their hair or because of their jewels or fancy clothes. Women should listen and learn quietly and humbly." I always thought that meant being suppressed and letting men rule and stomp all over you. But freedom is only a liberation to be the woman God wants us to be. I found that by losing myself in my mate, I found myself and he found himself. Christ tells us to reverence our husbands as the Lord. Pleasing our husbands pleases God, and we experience the joy of the Lord. This joy comes when we are doing the perfect will of God.

Sometimes I've wondered if submission has been stressed enough or too much. So few wives seem to know how to handle what they interpret to be freedom in Christ. Freedom in Christ does not make us independent of human needs.

The way we express our joy in the Lord will have a lot to do with our husband's acceptance or nonacceptance of us, and perhaps with his acceptance of Christ.

It is not carnal for a husband to feel threatened when his wife undergoes a complete personality change, when she is tuned in to spiritual things. It seems to her man to make her less than human. It's like having a wife and waking up one day to the fact he doesn't have her. He begins to rebel against this God who has taken his wife from him. It appears for awhile that he and God are in competition. When he rebels he is judged or condemned even more because he doesn't like or accept her new life-style.

A liberty which takes us out of reality and threatens another is not spiritual liberty. It may be a human release of spiritual ego.

We need to recall that our bodies are not ours, but our husbands. His body is not his, but ours. Paul told us not even to separate for fasting for a season except by mutual permission and agreement. (See 1 Cor. 7:5).

At a recent couples' retreat, many were sharing personal testimonies. In several cases men were sharing about a spiritual change they had noticed in their wives.

They said at first their wives seemed totally preoccupied, and they didn't like this change. But soon the wives discovered how to express and handle themselves in a less offensive manner. Each husband reported that his wife had become more compatible and, as one husband said, also more "patible." These husbands had been won by the chaste and discreet conversation of their wives. They stood tall and proud, knowing God for themselves. They said their wives released them to be themselves. Their wives stopped trying to make them over. That kind of freedom is convincing!

When Paul talks in Ephesians about our practical walk in the world and human relationships, he only speaks of submission after he has explained our exalted position in Christ. When we understand this position, we think of submission as service to Christ. It is looking at everyone else as being separate from Christ which gives us all our pain. Give the other person a break too. Let him be himself in the Lord. If he doesn't know the Lord, don't take the direct action. Love and accept him as he is. Let him see you have not moved out of reality. You are more real than ever. You are more sensitive to his needs. You don't have to be running day and night to be fulfilled. You are still his wife and need his manly lordship and protection. Sarah called Abraham "Lord."

Don't isolate yourself from your mate. Be more involved than ever with his dreams, his goals, and his needs as a man. Keep togetherness. Plan your times together. Keep child-like and natural about your love life. Let him know you need him to pray for you, while he's at work, sometime during the day. Set an hour when you can quietly pray for each other. Then thank him for praying.

A divorced man, who has since married, told me: "My wife of today appreciates my ability, and tells me right along; whereas my childhood sweetheart knew my weaknesses, and told me about them all the time. I like appreciation better."

God solidifies and unites families. Guard your homes.

5. FOR MEN ONLY

God made Adam and told him to take dominion. God's original plan was that Adam should rule over His world. He brought forth the animal kingdom and Adam named them all.

Then God saw Adam needed a helpmate, So he took Eve from Adam's side. Man was first, then the woman.

Our original parents—Adam and Eve—explain to us the pattern of the sexes today. Eve was beguiled by the serpent. Adam was persuaded by Eve. Beguilement and persuasion are two different things. Women can be led astray quickly by the deceit or conniving of evil. They become enchanted or charmed more easily than a man. A man is more logical in his conclusions.

A man's biggest temptation is a woman. He loves to please a woman, be admired by a woman, give to a woman. A woman has tremendous powers and, if she is honest, she will admit that her husband rises or falls according to her estimation of him. Almost every woman knows what it takes to make her man happy, if she is sensitive.

Whether it was in the garden that man began his subordinate role or not, certainly he lost his dominion of his inner as well as his outer world.

The Bible traces many times when a man buckled

under the dominating influence of a wife. Sarah influenced Abraham to take Hagar as his mistress, beginning a thousand generations of pain, as well as causing immediate agony to their home.

Rebekah persuaded her son, Jacob, to fool his father and steal the birthright from his brother.

Rachel caused trouble between her father and her husband, Jacob, because she took the idols from her father's house and hid them on her beast of burden.

Miriam caused trouble between Moses and Aaron because of her pride and haughty spirit concerning who was God's appointed leader.

Delilah persuaded Samson to disclose his secret of strength, causing the champion of Israel to lose his eyes and his freedom, bringing him into total disgrace.

Solomon's wives turned away his simple heart from the pure love of Jehovah.

Jezebel, the adulterous wife of Ahab, brought the pagan worship of Baal into the heart of God's country, causing sensuality and rampant promiscuity, not only in the land but in worship. Elijah, the most fearless of the prophets, defied King Ahab and the elements themselves (holding back the rain); yet Elijah ran terrified before the treacherous woman, Jezebel.

Herodias overrode Herod's godly fear of John the Baptist, and ordered his head cut off to appease her angry spirit.

The powers of a woman are beyond imagination. The history of the nations will prove that men have risen, fallen, or overthrown world empires at the persuasion of a woman.

Good women are traceable throughout history and the Holy Scriptures as well. Their good words, intuitions, chaste behaviors, and intense devotion have been the salvation of men and nations.

But even devout women are prone to use their very devotion and pinnacle over a man. It is never right for a woman or a man to dominate. Control over another's life, whether willful or unknowing, is wrong. A man was made to rule but his rule is the mantle of love, the kind of love that sent Christ to the cross to die for the sins of the world. Such a rule of love cannot hurt, nor deprive, nor take advantage of. It cannot smother the abilities or God-given creativity of the woman. It loves to see the other person reach their highest potential.

What happens when a woman uses her built-in powers to cripple a man? Then a man needs to assert his God-ordained leadership. She may rebel and resist his leadership, but the chances of her coming to God's perfect order and finding that perfect key to a good relationship are much greater than if the man submits to tantrums, scolding, pouting or nagging. If the husband comes under his wife's whip, he will likely be bewitched and cower all his life, mistrusting his own decisions and self-worth.

When a woman receives the Lord first, in a home, she often starts to coerce her husband to change. She often retreats into her world of books, new relationships, prayer meetings and Bible study. He then feels vengeful toward God who has seemingly broken up his home.

A woman who becomes more conversant about spiritual things can become a threat to a Christian husband. He is intimidated to pray, and he may feel he prays in the wrong way or that his method of prayer is, in some way, inferior to her kind of prayer. He concludes she's got a hot line to heaven because she tells

him so. Because he cannot shine in the spiritual world, he may seek to pour his strength into the secular world. Many men would rather give up than fight; and, since God is involved, they take a lot of guilt upon themselves.

The agression of the wife often intensifies, and she appears as the walking saint. Her husband becomes the spiritual tag-a-long. And, if he drops out altogether, the wife becomes the martyred saint; he, the target of the small prayer fellowships.

Because his wife has broken the perfect rhythm of God's order and because he has allowed himself to assume an inferior role, the husband is out of step—both in the church and in the home. His last defense is to lead in the secular world, if there is the slightest chance he can succeed there.

Many Christian women are reversing their dominating holds upon their husbands and their families. Their emotions break down under the pressures of self-appointed control. Being the weaker vessel, the responsibilities are too much for the woman and the game of superiority is no longer enamoring. Now she wishes to turn over the leadership of the home and family to him. She will try to give her husband the spiritual reins and urge him to take charge.

And what happens, so many times, in this situation where the dominant wife attempts to hand back to her husband the headship of their home? She finds that he is unaccustomed, shy, intimidated and insecure with this unfamiliar role. It would actually be easier to let her keep right on controlling. He has found a certain freedom in his bondage; he doesn't have to make difficult decisions or take responsibility. The cry of many such wives is, "How do I get my husband to take spiritual leadership and leadership in the home?"

I have only a one-word answer, "Slowly!"

But, if women were smart enough to get control in the first place, they are smart enough to start over. They will seize every opportunity to switch their role and read every book or help available.

Men who want to salvage their original God-given ego, who are endowed with the physical and emotional strength for leadership, will need to seize these reins and get in the driver's seat whether the saddle fits them or not. When a man's attempts to lead are awkward he needs to keep right at it. He has forfeited his birthright. Now that he has a chance to have it back he must conquer it like a cripple learning to walk again.

A woman eventually distrusts and disrespects a man she herself has whipped into conformity. Though she fights her husband's leadership role, something deep within her knows it's right.

If a man misuses his authority as lord of his house, he has aborted the perfect plan for the smooth functioning of his home and is no more happy than when his wife ruled. An abusive husband, insensitive to his wife's need for love, understanding and a sense of being needed has crushed his own flower garden and will live out his days unhappily.

Men, tell your wives you know how to drive a car. You can decide where to eat. You can pray and instruct the children. Step into your God-given roles and lead your families, your church and your world. We Christian women give you the reins. We want you to take them. You must take them in order for us to survive, spiritually.

Be kings on the throne, and we'll be queens at your side. Three cheers for men who rule with love and women who would have it be so!

6. YOU CAN BE AS HAPPY AS YOU WANT TO BE

When my husband and I returned home from a ten-day trip, we found the following note on our hall table. It was written by our married son, Steve, who collected the mail for us while we were gone.

"Dear Mom and Dad, Welcome home. I'm a very happy married man and I love my new home. But I love this home, too. I like to walk through these rooms. I like what I feel. I like the smell. I love you guys alot. I'm glad you're home. Love, Steve."

Homes radiate moods. They reflect the personalities of the people who live in them. We all have walked into places and felt tense and awkward. We've found it was hard to smile. It seemed as if our thoughts came slowly and our words were sort of mumbo-jumbo.

These moods are not always unpleasant, and we must *remember* that while we absorb moods *from* other people, we are equally creating moods for them.

We don't even have to say anything to create a mood. Spirit is something which cannot be completely housed in a body. I may know how a person feels about me without a word being spoken. S.D. Gordon, in his marvelous book, *Quiet Talks on Prayer*, says, "Hate is a spirit which can be felt thousands of miles away. Love is also a spirit which may be felt thousands of miles." Spirit knows no boundaries.

Homes carry the atmosphere of the people who reside in them; offices, the atmosphere of the people who work in them. Schools reflect the atmosphere that the students and administration create. Likewise, churches radiate the atmosphere of the people who worship there. It is our judging, our lack of love, our feelings of spiritual superiority, our critical fault-finding attitude, our religious prejudice, which puts the ice on any religious gathering, no matter how intent the worshipers may be.

Oswald Chambers, in his daily devotional, *My Utmost for His Highest*, says, "Spiritual truth is learned by atmosphere, not by intellectual reasoning."

The test of any truth, church doctrine or creed, is love. That brother who has out-loved me is my master, no matter what I profess.

The home which creates a mood or atmosphere to which you long to come is the home where you'll find the most love and trust, and where the acceptance of its members is not determined by their performance.

A husband will rush home to a loving, appreciative wife who thinks of his needs paramount to her own.

A child will run to the refuge of walls which are coated with praise, love, acceptance, and trust.

I receive letters from single people quite often. The normal desire of every human is companionship. I don't have to read far into most letters to find the single adult's most common problem: low self-esteem. At some point in life they have accepted the idea that they were inferior. By accepting that premise as a fact, anyone will eventually project a mood of insecurity and uncertainty. Instead of seizing opportunities boldly, they retreat from life. If a girl wants to be accepted, she must first accept herself. When we reject ourselves we become boring and unenthusiastic about life.

It takes effort on our part to be enthusiastic. Life will not hand us more than we put into it. If a girl will not take the time or make the effort to be available, and to be excited about life, she will have to pay the penalty of a lonely existence. Even with a beautiful face, a dull person can fade into the woodwork without being seen. Life gives to the person who helps himself to it.

Our daughter Ann had prayed for several years for the Lord to select her marriage partner. When she saw him, she had a strange feeling that this was the one! She wrote home and said, "What shall I do, Mom?" We exchanged letters and I gave her some tips on how I thought she might get his attention.

One day a letter arrived. "Well, Mom, I did it. I have a date this week with this neat guy."

He was a football player and was usually in a crowd so it wasn't easy for Ann to get him alone or drop her notebook in his path. Her letter went on to say that one day she sat down at the table with the football players and said innocently, "Is this where all the football jocks sit?" Needless to say, Ann created a mood of curiosity. And sure enough, her dream man followed her out and asked for a date. He fell madly in love with her within a few weeks. Today they are happily married—loving, playing, learning and growing together. If Ann had not created a happy enthusiastic mood, she might not have ever gained his attention.

Do you want to spruce up your home, your husband's return after work? Then act like it! Create a mood of of excitement, joy, agressiveness, enthusiasm. Don't let anyone be more exciting than you are. You are as happy as you want to be. It will take effort and unselfishness on your part to create a wholesome, happy mood.

You are creating a mood for your family, your church, your community, and your world. Radiate the happy moods, for in so-doing you will make yours and someone else's life worth living.

7. THE BONDAGE OF POSSESSIVENESS

All of us have a set of circumstances, familiar surroundings, a particular group of people or one person which gives our life a solidarity and makes us feel secure. This gives us comfort and, if it is removed from us, causes us pain and insecurity.

My husband gets attached to his chair. He has a fixed pattern for his light, his books, and the stand nearby for his coffee. I know better than to dabble too much with his nest. I work around his spot when I change the furniture. If I do change the location of his chair, all the accompanying surrounding objects go with it.

Most of us could survive a chair "change," but many of us can be destroyed over the breaking of dearer ties. Probably nothing is more needed than the ability to release the possessive holds on our loved ones.

Our daughter went to college 2000 miles away. She took me in her bedroom, just before leaving, and said, "I'd like to have a last prayer with you, Mother." She prayed, and thanked God for the trauma of the teen cycles we had come through together. We went out to the car, and there her father prayed and blessed the travelers. Ann rolled down the window of the car as it turned the corner, waved her hand, and said, "Thanks for my life!" If we had not held her loosely for 18 years, we may have had great difficulty in accepting her departure.

Ann was back to visit on New Years. She said, "You know, Mother, when you really give up your possessive holds on your children, God gives them back to you as friends."

Many of us do not love with open arms. Many couples who are married and have children are still under the control of a parent, very often the mother. Every decision is prefaced by a thought of Mother's approval or disapproval.

Such a bondage is unnatural and deprives the married companion of the needed trust they deserve. Because parents raise, feed, and clothe us in our early life we owe them love in our adult years. If parents release a child early, the child will not resent the attention and care sometimes needed by parents in later years. A parent should not put smothering demands on children.

A lazy, unmotivated child can often be traced to a mother who did everything for him. Many parents try to buy their children's love and are hated for it. It may bring some momentary pleasures but a love dependent on gifts is not love at all. Sooner or later the veneer of buying love and loyalty will be resented. A parent who wants to give a child all the things he never had, just because he can afford it, need not wonder that a child has a confused set of values.

Possessiveness repulses others. Strong possessiveness and attachments can affect our health because they create an imbalance. True love releases what it loves. My husband and I would rather see our children happy and fulfilled, with their mates, than clustered around us satisfying our needs. Our needs can be filled by giving ourselves away to others.

Release draws you to your own. Many young girls, while longing for the right mate, refuse to let go of one boyfriend for fear they will not find a better choice.

Toying with the emotions of a companion with whom they foresee no future can reap a harvest of unhappiness. It is unfair to keep the close attachment.

Trying to bend others to our will, while calling it love, is selfish possessiveness. Seeking to control another person's life directly or indirectly is wrong. If intensely practiced, it can produce depressions and is Satanically inspired. When prayers are prayed in an effort to change someone, it is important that we pray positive prayers for people or we only make negative affirmations. Affirmation means to "make firm." The Bible says, "Woe to them that make unrighteous decrees" (Isa. 10:1, *KJV*).

In order to grow, we must release all possessive holds. This is an important key. We must let go of what is in our hands in order to receive the new thing God is preparing for us.

At our first women's fellowship of the new year we spread our open hands, before the Lord, and prayed this prayer:

"Dear Lord, we are ready to let go of all the negatives of our life. We let go of all possessive holds. We let go of hurt, anger, pride, envy, poverty, bitterness, fear, self-pity. Go out insecurity, rejection, rebellion, sickness, criticism, judging, suspicion, unbelief, greed worry, unbelief! We let go of every negative.

"We receive from you, Lord, joy, peace, trust, fulfillment, money and happiness. We receive all our needs, met by you. Come in faith, free-flowing spirit, freedom, friends, self-worth, forgiveness of sins, forgiveness of others, and love."

Let go of possessive holds on others and pronounce

yourself free of the possessiveness of others. "If the Son sets you free, you will indeed be free—" (John 8:36).

8. RECLAIM YOUR SPIRITUAL PARENTHOOD

"If that were my child, he'd never do that!"

"If I had children, they'd certainly never talk that way."

And so, "Claiming themselves to be wise without God, they became utter fools instead" (Rom. 1:22).

There are an increasing number of family seminars these days. It seems God is raising up a host of enlightened men and women to lay a surer foundation for the home. It's refreshing to see young parents attending these seminars and taking a fresh look at God-given perspectives for their homes.

I must confess, I smart a little when the family laws are shared loud and clear. I smart for the parent who has raised his children to a teenage level or for the parent whose children have left the nest. "Why didn't I know this raising my children? What hope is there for me? The horse is already out of the barn!"

In one seminar a father said, "I don't know how I ever survived with the kind of father I had. No matter how much I hated my dad's methods of discipline, I have followed his pattern. Now, my son is repeating my performance even though he hated everything I represented. I am full of bitterness. My life is such a mess. I don't feel I can tell anyone about Christ. I've been a poor example of a Christ-filled life."

The wonderful thing about God is that He starts where we are, and He never gets through with us. Getting the sin problem settled is only a beginning. We will never be the finished product until we see the Lord face to face.

If we really want to clear the deck, God knows it and He will provide the opportunity.

Only when we humble ourselves before God will we gain the sweet presence and the peace of His indwelling Spirit. We must:

(1) Ask God to forgive us; (2) Ask others to forgive us; and (3) Forgive ourselves, which is always the most difficult task.

Be as honest as possible about the people you don't like, people who make you chafe. If you have committed definite sins against another person, seek to make things right.

Jesus said, "The evil prince of this world approaches. He has no power over me" (John 14:30). In God there is no darkness at all. If there is any darkness in you, this will hinder answers to your prayers.

Parents, never say, "It's too late." It is *never* too late! If you are suffering through painful problems involving your children, and your relationship with them, then agree with your mate to daily pray together for your children and for wisdom in giving parental guidance.

Stop praying negatively to God about your child. Pray affirmations of good things which you expect—by faith—to happen.

Write love notes to your child, whether you ever deliver them or not, they will change your whole mental attitude to one of love and trust rather than apprehension.

If your child doesn't live at home, but at a distance, think loving thoughts about him. Love is a spirit. Love travels! Miles away, someone's heart can be refreshed by your loving, trusting thoughts.

Visualize your child in a new, happy, loving way, giving no thought to appearances.

Release all the concepts of mistrust and condemnation. Remind Satan that he no longer has a hold on you. Allow a cleansing of your own life, past and present.

Then think back to the time your child's birth, and review each negative memory. Reclaim that damaging impression and claim the blood of Jesus for it.

Then praise God for the completed restoration of your child to the fold of His love and the family unit until it is visibly manifest.

"Dear Lord Jesus, we release all personal claims on our own life. We eradicate from our hearts any darkness the devil may find to claim.

"We ask forgiveness for past errors when we have hurt, hindered, or judged another person. We forgive all the people whose influence has given rise to the unhappy and unfulfilled person we now are.

"We will gladly follow through on personal restitution which would free us or another person without doing injury to their present circumstances.

"We freely let go of all negative thoughts about our children. We ask forgiveness for ignorantly adding to their lack of self-worth and any present hostility. We ask you to make all the crooked paths straight.

"We wish to view all people, and especially our children, with love. We withdraw our condemning spirit. We will bless, not curse, our children and will depend on you to restore our spiritual parenthood. We praise you, and thank you. Amen."

9. WILL THE PERFECT PARENT STAND UP?

We all start out to be the perfect parent. And perfect parents ought to produce perfect children. We have all the answers until Junior breaks the sound barrier; and every month we get a little quieter, a little less verbal, and much more humble.

Not only do we want to raise Junior for the Lord, but desire to fill the basic yearning to "produce after our kind."

The old adage, "Hindsight is better than foresight," is certainly true. It takes a heap of growing not to buckle under the pressure of consciously (or unconsciously) trying to make Junior the model of perfection.

In rearing our children, we wore James 1:5 rather threadbare: "If you want to know what God wants you to do, ask, and he will gladly tell you, for he is always ready to give a bountiful supply of wisdom to all who ask him." The teen years were especially stimulating to our faith. If Mom and Dad can agree perfectly on the decisions made, it's a big help.

I must admit that, in our marriage, we didn't always totally agree. I learned, however, through trial and error that my husband's judgments were usually best. I learned to respect my husband's position as head of our home. God's chain of command explicitly says that the husband should rule his house, love his wife; and that a woman is to submit to this leadership. As a Christian, the wife will either submit to her husband's leadership, or she will wreck her home, her husband's self-image, and her own nerves.

The most important thing, at any age, is to keep communication open—between husband and wife, between parents and children. I am grateful that our son and daughter, in their growing up years at home, always included us in their lives. I recall many times when our son would stretch his six-foot frame across the end of our bed, when he came in, as he shared with us some exciting news of the activities of his day.

Jesus Christ was very natural at our house. As a family, we didn't have heavy, long devotional times. I kept a notebook of favorite Scriptures, and we discussed one verse each morning at breakfast. We memorized the verse and applied it to some situation the children were having at school. Sometimes we even spent three or four days on one verse. When the children came home I'd ask how the Scripture verse had worked for them that day. They learned to depend on a Scripture for every occasion. When they found themselves in a new situation, facing a new set of problems, we'd search the Scriptures together for the solution.

I believe it's not the quantity of time spent with your children, but the *quality* that counts. Do they feel rushed in your presence or do they feel, at that moment, that they're the most important persons in the world?

On weekdays, the visitation pastor at our church wakes his two boys early and jogs with them. Then they go out for breakfast together. He sees very little of them until the weekend, but the times spent together are very special. One of his sons, when asked by his sixth-grade teacher, "What one thing would hurt you more than anything else in the world?" answered with this response: "For my dad to quit the ministry." What a testimony! Here's a father whose calling necessitates long hours away from home; yet he gives his sons "quality" time, and he's leaving the imprint of Jesus Christ on his children's lives.

One of the common sins of parents is to withold approval when their child fails to "come through" properly. Witholding approval from a child because he isn't satisfying you is like refusing to shine a light into a dark room because it's too dark. To withold approval is to short-circuit the flow of love into a child's life, and to deprive him of the opportunity to be inspired and restored to the fold of love and acceptance once more. Showing approval, on the other hand, is like unleashing an atom! It's impact is explosive.

A mother complained one day in a counseling session that her boy was "impossible." After listening for some time, the counselor finally asked, "Does he do anything well?"

"Oh yes, he can make boats."

"Then start with boats!" the counselor suggested.

Willing to give it a try, the mother waded through the disaster area which her son called his "room," to the beginning of a new boat creation. She watched for a while, as her son glued the minute pieces of the model in place, and began to tell him he must be a genius. Day after day, she waded through his room, to the boat tinkerer, to see the genius at work. One afternoon, to her pleasant surprise, she discovered he'd actually hung up his shirt. She said, "Thanks, son that's nice of you." And, in a short period of time, the boy was sitting beside his mother in church.

Stop trying to make your child a carbon copy of yourself. He may grow to know God a lot better if he feels that you trust his decisions, even though he may conflict with some of those things which you consider "convictions."

When it comes to rearing children, no human being has all the answers; but there's always some place to start. You can find some reason to show your child approval, to begin to close that communication gap. Only when your child senses your approval will he gain feelings of self-worth and be open to your love. There is no stronger bond than love.

10. DEVELOP YOUR CHILD'S FEELINGS OF SELF-WORTH

In the past few years, both the church and the secular world have become aware of the importance of individual self-worth. We may be converted while possessing feelings of low self-esteem, but we may not aspire to the abundant life Jesus promised us without acknowledging our own worth.

While counseling a young girl, only married a few months, I was saddened to hear that her new husband was in the midst of a nervous breakdown. His family had kept a dominant control over his entire life. Every decision had been preluded by their approval or disapproval, including his place of employment (in their lucrative business). Being married had not lessened their control. Because of his inability to cope with life and trust his own decisions, this young man had relinquished all personal trust and allowed them to commit him to a hospital for psychiatric help.

There is no unsolvable problem. Praise God for that! But the process may be slow in coming. So much could have been salvaged in this young man's life, as well as multitudes of others, if parents only had applied some good sense and practical Christian principles.

Feelings of self-worth cannot be attained by six easy lessons, but they can be reprogrammed anytime. If you don't have children, perhaps you have grandchildren, nieces or nephews. Or, maybe, you teach a Sunday school class. Whatever your sphere of influence, I hope you will be able to apply some of the 20 pointers, to follow, with anyone who needs a healthy dose of self-worth.

1. *View your child as a person.*

It's easy to forget a little child is really a person. His feelings, and your responses to him are making lasting impressions on him. Try to imagine yourself in your child's shoes. Look at the situation through his eyes. If you do, you'll find there's nothing unimportant in his world, and you will relate to him with a gentler, kinder, more understanding spirit.

2. *Develop a fascination with the world around you.*

People who have developed a wholesome excitement for little things are interesting people. Our son has an amazing ability to recognize things in nature that I completely overlook. I used to think he was just imagining that he saw a deer flit through the woods, a snake crawl through the grass, or a rabbit hop behind a tree. While traveling he would become breathless at the sight of a creek, or a turtle, as we whizzed by in our automobile. But he wasn't joking. He really was attuned to nature, and it seemed to be performing just for him. And, to this day, he has never lost his childlike wonder with nature. A mother can share this fascination for every little thing, every new experience, with her child. He will think she's the greatest, if she does.

3. *Turn your child loose, for independent decisions, as soon as possible.*

The younger the child, the better to trust him with responsibility. Instead of saying, "Be careful when you cross the street or a car will run you down," say, "I'm so glad you're grown up and look both ways when you cross the street. You're somebody Mother can really trust." Instead of instilling fear, you have instilled confidence. He will need this for more serious decisions.

4. *Develop trust.*

Let your child know you believe in him. My husband's favorite song, after he became a Christian, stated: "I would be true for there are those who trust me. I would be pure for there are those who care." The confidence of others, especially your parents, is a tremendous guiding and restraining force in temptation. If a child is not trusted by parents or peers, he will likely fulfill their expectations, lack confidence in himself and his decisions.

5. *Save your serious judgements for serious matters.*

A child who hears a parent constantly correct him over trifles will never know the difference when he does commit a more serious blunder. He soon tunes out the constant nagging and honestly doesn't hear it. Most little problems can be met with a healthy sense of humor and an intelligent conversation. Many mothers are nitpicky about small matters, and too often the child gets the brunt of parental frustration. No wonder he tunes us out.

6. *Avoid making your child feel guilty.*

While a child is developing, avoid making him feel guilty or awkward about his physical or emotional changes. As he participates in the teen process of acquiring an independence from you, let him do so without blame. Avoid sarcasm and teasing about his changing shape and his altered feelings.

7. *Plant confidence.*

Your child needs you to implant thoughts within him that he can achieve whatever worthy goal he sets his mind to. Never surround your child with negative thoughts which stress his lack of ability. Mrs. Einstein withstood all of her son's early teachers when they claimed he was ignorant. She insisted, in his presence, that Albert was a genius. Needless to say, she won! Albert Einstein became the world's mental champion, discovering the mathematical concept of relativity. Psychologists have proven that I.Q.'s have actually improved because of a mother's continual emphasis on her child's abilities, rather than on his limitations.

8. *Release your married child.*

Releasing your child should begin long before marriage. If you have done your homework well, you will have released him—with confidence—very early. A possessive control of your child inhibits his developing self-hood. When he sets up a natural resistance to our control, we usually take it for rebellion. If treated as a rebellious child, he seeks acceptance and trust elsewhere—in fact, anywhere he can get it.

Many parents are hurt because their children pay little attention to them after marriage. Perhaps the relationship is no longer wholesome, free, relaxed. If the married child still feels the parental strings of control, he will either succumb and develop increased feelings of inferiority, or will become bitter and thoughtless toward the parent. Jesus said we were to leave our parents and cleave to our mate (Matt. 19:5, KJV). When we do, it's most likely that we will be able to honor and love our parents the way the Bible says we should.

9. *Spend quality time together.*

Some mothers are under bondage, feeling that they must spend all their time with their children. I believe the quality of time spent with our child is more essential than the actual amount of time itself. There are times when our children need us more than others. Coming home from school to an empty house can add to a child's insecurity. It's important that some special time is given, each day, to hear him out. Be interested in what he's doing. Have some advice on how to solve some of his problems. Take time to listen. Take time to play as well as pray.

10. *Don't provoke your children to wrath.*

This is clearly commanded by God's Word. Every child needs proper restraint. But, often, the correction we give is the result of a sudden outburst of our own frustration, and does not convey the real concern we feel for our child. A youngster needs to know why he's being corrected. He needs to understand that a loving mother or father cannot overlook behaviors or attitudes which will ultimately harm his life. If we parents rush into correction we will probably make our child angry; if we pause to explain, we'll probably make him sorry. Angry children become bitter children.

Be in control when you administer correction to your child. The Bible says, in Colossians 3:21, "Provoke not your children to anger lest they be discouraged" (*KJV*) or, as *The Living Bible* states, "Don't keep on scolding and nagging your children, making them angry and resentful" (Eph. 6:4). If a child's spirit is broken in his tender years, he will carry with him—into adulthood— feelings of inferiority and rejection. Sometimes these feelings of self-rejection eat on the adult, in the cancer of unforgiveness. I was once told, by a 60-year-old-lady, that she still couldn't forgive her mother for beatings she had received as a child, at the age of two. It was vivid in her memory, though her mother had been dead for a number of years.

11. *Guard against giving a child a "poor" image.*

Not all families are endowed with the same financial assets. Prosperity, however, is more than money. It is an attitude or spirit. It is important for a child not to think of himself as "poor." Talk frequently with your child about how God supplies your family's financial needs, and seize opportunities to point out the visible evidences of His miracles. Constant references to "lack" of financial resources tend to multiply that lack, in the eyes of your child. Though your family may never claim to have money to spare, you can instill, within the child, a sense of security by accentuating the positive—showing thanks for the way in which God so adequately provides for your needs.

12. *A child needs constant praise and appreciation.*

Observe how fast a plant grows by proper watering, feeding and care. Just as that plant—which requires regular loving care in order to thrive—a child needs our constant praise. Approval is like a big dose of vitamins. It's a shot which blasts loose limitations and feelings of inferiority. A child will do almost anything to keep the approval of a parent. Approval allows a child to come to the peak of his performance. Lack of approval makes him feel inferior, stupid and inadequate. If you wait for your child to satisfy all of your desires before you compliment him, you will never have the opportunity. Appreciation assures him of his ability and gives him a desire to reach higher. Start with anything good about him—and praise him. Soon you will find there are many more good abilities and qualities for which you can offer praise and appreciation.

13. *Develop a feeling that you need him and like to be with him.*

I think the greatest compliment either of our children has paid us is when they say, "I really like being with you," or "You are fun to be with."

On the other hand, children need to know we parents need them, too. Sometimes it doesn't hurt to let a child know you have a problem and need him to help solve it. My husband and I often went to our children to ask them to pray for us. This show of confidence in them tends to make children more responsive and responsible persons. You are saying, "I trust your prayers for me."

Everyone needs to be needed. Ask your children's advice about important decisions. Make major decisions a family affair, always with the knowledge that, after accumulating all the facts, the head of your house (the husband) will make the ultimate final decision. Your children like to be included in family decisions.

14. *Keep a healthy image of yourself.*

It undermines a child's sense of security to hear either

parent cut himself down. To speak of yourself as stupid, unlearned, ignorant, ugly, fat, poor or disliked is to tell a child he has inherited a very inferior life for himself. In our family, we determined that our children would know, at a very young age, that they were special. We let them know God must have loved them a lot! We stacked up the opportunities and never acknowledged the limitations.

15. *Avoid judging people.*

All children will receive their share of cruel comments and experiences from other children, and even teachers. They need to be aware of the hard and fast, "Sowing and Reaping Law." Children won't be so quick to return evil or to institute it if they know they will receive it back in due measure. My daughter used to say, "No, I better not say that or someone will say it about me."

When a child is hurt unjustly, it is wise to attempt to prevent them from immediately judging that individual who inflicted the pain. Here are some suggested pacifiers:

(1) "Your teacher probably had a very hard day."
(2) "Perhaps she had a fight at home."
(3) "Maybe someone's sick. Let's pray for her."
(4) "Maybe your friend is jealous of you because he needs to have someone to love him like you do. Let's pray for him."
(5) "Maybe someone has made them feel inferior so they must try to hurt someone who's not. Let's pray they won't feel like that."

If you take your child's hurt personally, with them, you have compounded their problem. The Bible says, "Bless . . . and curst not." (Rom. 12:14, *KJV*). "Don't criticize, and then you won't be criticized. For others will treat you as you treat them" (Matt. 7:1, 2). The sooner children learn these principles, the better.

16. *Develop a healthy attitude toward the opposite sex.*

Mothers who tell their children that sex is dirty and that all children of the opposite sex cannot be trusted are sowing serious seeds of maladjustment. Being interested in the opposite sex, at a proper age, is a natural part of life. Marital sex is certainly a natural function in life. The inhibitions of married people are usually carry-overs of early training. Your children need frank, honest answers about life, dating, marriage. Don't press more information on them than they are ready for. Their questions indicate what they are getting ready to hear. Probably no natural appetite has been so abused, nor caused as much grief, as sex. Mothers, don't dominate your children, boys especially; and fathers, take an active interest in your child's development. A weak father can produce very confused children when it comes to identifying sexual roles. The family is God's institution. Prepare your child to understand and accept the sex act in marriage for what God planned that it should be—the perfectly normal, loving, physical union between marriage partners when they become totally one with their mate. Until the time of their marriage, teach your children to balance sexual purity with an increasing awareness and awakening of their God-given sexual appetites.

17. *Say, "I am sorry."*

Never become too right, too exact, too stubborn, or too brittle to say, "I am sorry." Every parent will make mistakes. Since these mistakes are apparent to our children anyway, we might as well say so. God always gives grace to the humble, but resists the proud. (See James 4:6 (KJV). The Spirit can only bear witness to truth. When our actions betray our words, there's no use to pretend. Tell your child the truth. If you reacted or did something contrary to principle, say so. He will love you for it, and will have a living example of the way he is to react when he's done wrong.

18. *Place proper priority on beauty.*

Every child wants to be beautiful. Every child is beautiful. However, some children have more outward beauty than others. If you are blessed with a very outwardly beautiful child, you will need to help him develop proper priorities. I have seen beautiful people totally unbalanced because top priority was placed on their outward appearance. A beautiful child often becomes a status symbol for a parent. If the inward beauty of the child is not the main emphasis, he will be hated. People will be jealous of him, and he will not possess enough inner security to hold him up. Beauty with inward love is a wonderful combination; but outward beauty without love is a snare. If a child is not as outwardly beautiful as others, build on his abilities as his crowning asset. There are beautiful features about him than can be acknowledged.

Sometimes parents take crooked teeth for granted, not knowing that when their child is older he may actually refuse to smile because he's embarrassed. Both of our children wore braces; and both have since thanked us, repeatedly, for having it done. Correcting crooked teeth is a legitimate need, and God will help you to finance it.

Our society is weight conscious! While we parents don't need to starve our youngster in order to create string bean figures, we do need to teach our children good nutritional habits. Sometimes it may seem cute to see a small child indulge, and grow plump; but allowing our children too much sugar can create a sweet craze which will follow them through life. Obesity can produce psychological damage, in both children and adults.

Whatever your children's gifts, tell them they're beautiful! And you will see the results: increased amounts of beauty, both inward and outward.

19. *Don't compare your child with other children.*

No two children are alike so we cannot, and should not, expect the same performance from one as we do the other. How often counselors hear these words: "Mom liked my brother or my sister best"; "I was never as good at sports as my brother, so my parents never paid much attention to me"; "I wasn't as smart as the rest of the kids"; "I was the black sheep of the family"; or, "My mother never thought I could do anything right."

One of two sisters was beautiful. The other was average. This second sister suffered rejection because her family constantly reminded her that her sister got all the looks! Her emotional rejection became a deep, inward scar. The sisters grew up, and were married, and eventually each girl turned her offspring against the others. Each mother tried to make her children more beautiful, smarter, and more popular than her sister's children. One of these mothers even beat her child in an attempt to make him excel. His personality became introverted and emotionally warped.

Children must be allowed to be themselves, and should be accepted and loved for what they are. God has made each of us unique, and we please Him when

we accept and appreciate the unique qualities of our
children (or anyone else).

20. *Pray with your child and apply the Scriptures to his
     life.*

Every problem faced by you or your child has a
scriptural answer. The sooner your child realizes God's
power to hear and answer his prayers, the sooner he will
respond to a loving God. Never put God in the
punishment role for something the child has done
wrong. As he matures he may appropriate the discipline
of God; but it is important, as a young child, that he
knows a God of love. He should feel that the most
natural thing to do, in a difficulty, is to pray. If he sees
you pray and get answers, he will assume that's the
normal way to go. Apply the Bible to his needs. In 2
Timothy 3:15, Paul said of Timothy, "From a child
thou hast known the holy scriptures" (*KJV*). And at 12
years of age, Jesus astonished the scribes with his
knowledge and understanding of the Scriptures (see
Luke 2:42-47). Once learned, the Scriptures are never
forgotten. They may submerge for awhile, but they will
surface again. "Teach a child to choose the right path,
and when he is older he will remain upon it." (Proverbs
22:6).

Whatever age your child may be, it's never too late to
improve his self-image. If you've already impaired it,
ask God to forgive you, and begin to change it now.
God will be there to help you.

Part II

Your Attitudes

Part II

11. COPING WITH GLOOM

Have you ever started out a day feeling fresh, renewed in body, spirit and emotions? You had a good talk with God and tucked a promise in your mind and said to yourself, "Nothing can go wrong, nothing can go wrong."

Then you got your first telephone call, or you arrived at the office. Someone was just waiting with a tale of woe. Sometimes it affects you personally, your family, your church, your job or something else for which you are responsible. There's a moment of terror, then you begin again to get fortified. David, the psalmist, said, of the righteous man who fears and trusts in God: "He does not fear bad news, nor live in dread of what may happen. For he is settled in his mind that Jehovah will take care of him" (Psa. 112:7). The person who builds his life on happenings can be shattered in a moment. The person who builds on principle, is a fixed one and cannot be intimidated by negative minds.

One of my favorite authors said, "Nothing, even death, can hurt me. I've already been to my own funeral and have come back in the Alive."

How are we to cope with gloomy people or threatening happenings? To utter, or to listen to morbid, unwholesome talk can do the human being no good. It is a gross sin to talk discouragingly to souls hungering for hope.

Some people don't know better. We can forgive them. But when a person knows better, he violates the perfect rhythm of life and should be ashamed of killing hope and happiness in someone else. It's like putting poison in the cup of the one who asks for water.

Some people feel with a sense of righteousness, that they must fight the world. They are anti-life. Christ came to make us pro-life, not anti-life. All the changes which the world labels as progress are not necessarily wrong.

If you want to turn your children off, just tell them the way it was 30 years ago. Tell them how you walked two miles to and from school. Tell them how you worked eight hours a day when you were 14. Tell them what time you came in at night, and what rules you lived by as a child. They come equipped with a built-in "shut-off" button. Mentally, or verbally, they'll respond with a shrug, "That's tough!"

Life progresses and is always NOW. God is always now. Don't concentrate on glories of the past—days gone by. Recognize God's presence in your world and in your circumstances *today*, and your spirit will be revived and quickened. When I think of tomorrow, I know it will be "now" for Him, and He will have a plan for that day as well. Nothing will ever catch God off guard.

Recognize God's presence in the "now's" of your life, and gloom will evaporate. You'll be ready for the moment at hand.

If we are attuned to gloomy thoughts, we need to set up an expectation of something else.

If we are habitually saying, "I don't like that," try reversing your attitude to, "I like that." After about one week you might be able to say, "I love that!"

Instead of greeting our new day with fear or apprehension, try saying, "I can't wait to see what is in store for me today!"

If you dread the ring of the telephone because it's brought you pain in the past, say, "I wonder who's calling me with good news?"

If you think your age is a burden, try saying, "I anticipate age 35, 45, 55 or 65 with enthusiasm."

Jesus said, "Do you believe?" (John 9:35). What are you believing in? If you are believing you'll be blessed, prospered, healed, comforted, loved, *you will be*. What do you believe?

When Jesus ascertained the object of a woman's faith He said, "Your faith has made you well" (Matt. 9:22, *NASB*). He could have said His faith had done it, but He didn't; He said it was the *believer's* faith.

We can create an attitude of expectancy by our words, our thoughts, and our actions. Faith which is not acted upon is not faith at all.

Jesus always addressed the Father with an anticipation of the good already received. "Father, thank you for hearing me." (John 11:41).

"Listen to me!" Jesus said in Mark 11:24, "You can pray for anything, and if you believe you have it; it's yours!" We must anticipate the thing we desire or pray for.

This expectation gives us an unmistakable air of authority. If we expect results from our word, we get what we say. If we don't, we won't. If we understand this power, we attract and experience what we steadily expect. What we accept internally must appear externally.

Most of us have some false misconceptions which we

must give up before we can believe what is true. Even false beliefs give us some security, so we cling to them, afraid that if we let them go we'll be left dangling with nothing. But faith demands a lunge, a leap. You must

bet your life to win. Faith is not an experiment. It's tangible. Faith is a substance though it's unseen. It is an evidence of something sure to follow. If we entertain false concepts, this can bring about harmful relationships, sickness, rash decisions and even premature death.

"Your faith has saved you" (Luke 7:50). Your faith not only may save your soul but your life, your family, your church, your neighbor, your business. The faith to puncture the gloomy bubble which surrounds you begins in your mouth.

"For salvation that comes from trusting Christ—which is what we preach—is already within easy reach of each of us; in fact, it is as near as our own hearts and mouths" (Rom. 10:8). If you express your positive expectations, by faith, on your lips, soon your inner world will swing into harmony with what your mouth is saying.

You may have said, "It's hopeless, it will never be different."

Or if you desire to change, you can. Express your desire: "It's not hopeless! Circumstances can change!" All power in heaven and earth will come rushing in upon the man or woman who will dare to defy his negative, gloomy world. When your inner world of thoughts and attitudes has broken through to light, your outer world will naturally follow. Your faith can make you whole. You can cope with gloom.

12. FAITH IS "SETTING THE DIAL"

Some television programs I like more than others. I rather enjoyed the Mary Tyler Moore show. I didn't particularly care about what came before or after, but I usually viewed Mary Tyler Moore. Her show aired on Saturday nights at 7 p.m. As the clock approached seven, very often I would turn the dial to the correct channel, and then go about my work. I didn't run back and forth to the television set to see if it had jumped channels. I didn't adjust and readjust the TV color. I didn't stand by the clock to see if was still ticking until 7:00. I didn't reread the TV Guide to be sure I'd read it correctly the first time. I had set the television dial, so I forgot about it!

Faith is like that. It works effortlessly! And I'm learning a little more every day to not make such a fuss about it. The fuss I make over my forthcoming answers to prayer can actually be acting out unbelief.

Once I make a bold stand or declaration that I believe God for something, I have a mental picture or a scene upon the screen of my mind. It is done! But it often takes time to work out God's plan. Many of us do not consider the time element required in answers to prayer, so we fall back into unbelief and think we must have done something wrong.

Some of us need to stop trying to make our prayers be answered. We need to stop *trying* to be converted and *be* converted. We need to stop *trying* to be filled with the Spirit and *be filled* with the Spirit.

Just believe for answers and start enjoying the journey. Many of us are waiting for our answer to prayer to be happy. We wait for some new religious experience to be happy.

Nowhere does God say try to believe or try to be saved. Your original decree of faith has become a sturdy bridge and the picture must ultimately appear. From the decisive moment of faith, a powerful current is working beneath the surface of our lives. It works quietly and surely. Once the seed is planted, the Holy Spirit works ceaselessly and effortlessly.

You may wonder how soon results will appear. When we set our dial of faith, results arrive at once! At first, our reaction may be vague, but by feeding our faith with the Word and watering it with continual affirmations, the recognition of what God is doing gets clearer and clearer. Practically all conversion is like this. The experience is enjoyed before it can be explained. The blind man said, when cross-examined by the Pharisees, "I was blind, and now I see." (John 9:25). He didn't know all the ramifications of his healing, but he was certain of the reaction to the Master's touch. God's Word tells us to "Quietly trust yourself to Christ your Lord and if anybody asks why you believe as you do, be ready to tell him, and do it in a gentle and respectful way" (1 Pet. 3:15). But, if that were required for our initial act of faith, most of us would have never been converted. Our heart comes first and our head follows. If Nicodemus could not understand the nature of conversion, we probably wouldn't either, unless we can explain the wind blowing.

All light and truth are vague, in the beginning, but when embraced, are certain.

A few years ago my husband led a businessman to the Lord. On his way out of the office, Don thought to himself, "I sure hope that took!" It had seemed so matter-of-fact. Yet, the young business executive later reported that after about two hours a peace began to settle in, and the divine awareness of his own conversion took over. Unable to understand the full impact of his initial act of faith, this businessman found that now—years later—he's able to explain his conversion experience and to help others to find Christ.

Sometimes, following conversions, there are only small indications that a change has taken place. Perhaps you feel like making an apology. You feel kinder and more peaceful under pressure. You are more sensitive of others and less selfish. Since change is occurring from within, eventually your inner change will begin to be reflected favorably in your outward activities. All of life takes on a fresh look. Your relations with people have less static. The inner power increases and you become a magnet for good. It's like a river—once divided by many islands—which finally flows together. Your faith becomes an indominable onrushing force.

If there is a Satanic interference with your vision or answer to prayer, stare it down with unflinching eyes. It will have no power over you except the power you give it by recognition. "Give no opportunity to the devil" (Eph. 4:27, RSV). If you transfer your gaze to the interference you will become charmed by it and the real truth will become more obscure. Peter and John affixed their gaze with a look of faith upon the cripple at the Temple gate called the Gate Beautiful. Unapologetically they looked at him intently, and then Peter said, "Look here!" (Acts 3:4). They gazed down the evil disease as though it didn't exist. "I command you in the name of Jesus Christ of Nazareth, walk!" (See Acts 3:6-8). Jesus faced death, disease, sin, demons, and angry waves in exactly the same manner.

When interference comes there is a temptation to forfeit the original hope or dream. Though we appear outwardly peaceful, we need a rebellious sort of courage to endure. You must abandon any bridge which would take you back to familiar ground before you glimpse the promised land. A song the old-timers used to sing was, "Every bridge is burned behind me. Every bridge is burned behind me. Every bridge is burned behind me. I won't turn back." No matter how unfamiliar the road ahead, we dare not turn back.

You must be convinced the prize is there ahead. If this persuasion is strong enough, you'll enjoy the journey as much as the arriving.

On Mt. Sinai, God met with Moses and gave him the plan for the construction of the tabernacle. Many setbacks lay just ahead of Moses, but he never lost sight of the instruction and experience he had on the mount. His life, his vision, the tabernacle were all built on that original high hour or revelation. Build your life patterns from your highest hours.

If you are in the process of giving birth to something new and exciting in your life, you have set the dial. The hour will come, when there will be a thousand distractions. Keep the dial set and enjoy the journey. The answer will come!

13. THE PARALYSIS OF FEAR

Two Christians face the same tragedy. One becomes depressed and defeated, the other draws closer to God. Why?

I asked this question of a Sunday School class recently, and almost without exception the response was, "attitude."

Yes, attitude does make the difference! To carry to thought a bit further, we might ask: But why do some people have better attitudes than others? (In fact, we have to admit that some Christians have a poorer attitude than some non-Christians.) I would contend that attitudes are the results of "grace" or "choice." We choose many of our moods and reactions. However, a deeper walk with God will inevitably produce better moods.

Many Christians feel let down when threatening circumstances surround them, such as: money, health, or emotional problems. They allow negative thoughts and behaviorisms to take root, such as: prayerlessness, worry, selfishness, and coldness of heart.

Such attitudes come from the person who is living at the circumference and not at the center of God's will for his or her life.

In Exodus 14:1-14 the Israelites were being pursued by Pharaoh's armies. They had observed ten dramatic instances of the evidence of God's miraculous intervention, but even observing miracles didn't sustain them in a crisis. Nothing but a present awareness of Christ and implicit trust in His purposes will sustain us in the furnace of afflictions.

Pharaoh observed the situation and said, "They are wandering aimlessly in the land; the wilderness has shut them in" (Exod. 14:3, NASB).

How often the deafening roar of the enemy comes to our ears when there's trouble on every side, and we feel "shut in the wilderness."

When confronted with the Pharaoh's pursuit, the Israelites reacted in fear:

1. They were afraid.

2. They wanted to turn back to a lesser light, a familiar path, and slavery.

3. They blamed God's servant, Moses, for their trouble.

Only a giant in the faith could have stilled the fearful, condemning voices of millions of Jews, with the thundering hoofbeats of Pharaoh's horses pounding over desert sands, spurred on by an angry militia.

Moses, invested with boldness, dealt with fear in the only possible way at such an hour. He took charge! Sometimes there is no time to pray, to run to the Bible, to seek out your pastor or spiritual counselor. Moses took charge of his own fears and millions of others as he commanded: "Don't be afraid. Just stand where you are and watch, and you will see the wonderful way the Lord will rescue you today" (Exod. 14:13).

The command was clear and crisp, "Don't be afraid." Sometimes you must speak audibly to your fears. "Be still! Stop!"

His next command was to "Stand where you are . . . " Don't do anything, Moses admonishes. What you do in panic will probably be wrong. Force yourself and your emotions to "Be still!" Don't make any hasty decisions or commit a spurious act. Wait! Your haste may cause irreparable damage.

Thirdly, he set up an expectation. "Just stand where you are and *watch,* and you will see the wonderful way the Lord will rescue you today." It is staggering to see what one person in command can do when indwelt by God.

How many storms could you quiet if you caught your

rampant fears, your negative imaginings; became quiet; then took command.

Did God let Moses down? Never! God will never let his servant down. The sea parted for the Israelites to walk across dry sod while the Egyptians plunged to their death in the Red Sea. Israel saw the great work the Lord did and feared the Lord and believed Him and His servant Moses.

Norman Grubb, our dear friend, once said that he and his wife, when faced with an option of which side to take, always stood with the man of intense loyalty and faith in God, with daring acts of courage, even though at the time they couldn't visualize his vision.

Fear is an experience associated with a momentary sense of frustration, and feelings of imminent danger— of being cut off from peace and safety. Since God doesn't send these feelings, the source must be evil; and since this evil is coming from us, then we must have need of further cleansing. With the Christian, the need for cleansing is seldom in the surface. But as we tap a deeper level, these things are soon surrendered.

God says, "I have not given you the spirit of fear, but of power and of love and of a sound mind" (see 2 Tim. 1:7).

We can often rise to victory in a crisis but fail to regulate our lives in small matters. This is a daily process.

"Fear always contains some of the torture of feeling guilty." Since the Bible says, "Fully-developed love expels every particle of fear" (1 John 4:18, *Phillips*), we should press on to this grace. "Fear not" is as much a command as, "Be filled with the Spirit" (Eph. 5:18, *KJV*).

Release the fear of losses. Release the tight hold on people, opinions, and health. Surrender your tense, aggressive, possessive holds which are constantly vulnerable to a thousand instant changes. There is only one certainty: your oneness with Jesus Christ. Nothing else is permanent or secure.

Prayer:
"Dear Lord Jesus, Please take out this hidden part of me which responds so quickly to fear, anger, and frustation. I need you to cleanse my subconscious mind which houses these sudden responses. I claim perfect love which casts our fear. I will not be afraid. I will be still. I will take charge. I will allow no fear to have dominion over me. I am not separate. I am part of an indestructible whole. I am a spiritual being and I am joined to the Lord. Thank you for this deliverance. Amen."

14. CAN A CHRISTIAN LIVE FREE OF ANGER

Yes, but not without patience. Some Christians only express anger in a mild form, which is irritation. They can succeed without explosions of anger.

Sometimes unstrung nerves are a result of wrongdoing. Sometimes anger or irritability is a result of poor health. Whatever the cause, anger is a misfortune and any help to the sufferer will be appreciated.

I would like to share 15 ways one can deal with the anger or irritability habit:

1. If a person's unstrung nerves are due to poor health, very often rest is the best antidote. Rest is not an unspiritual way to handle some problems. Rest was

God's prescription for Elijah after fighting the Lord's battles. He became depressed over Jezebel's intensity to take his life. Fatigue and pressure gave way to depression. God not only refreshed Elijah by rest, but by feeding him. Proper eating habits enable the mind and emotions to maintain their stability. A touchy, faultfinding disposition may be put away if you honestly desire to do so. Make sure you have a desire to change and then set your will in that direction.

2. If you refuse to express a passion, it dies. When we were first married, my husband would always ask me to wait until I had slept all night before I gave someone my vented feelings. Invariably, by morning, the urge to "let go" seemed unimportant. If anything, the desire to express my vehemence had disappeared. So, count to 100 or stop to think it over first.

3. Tell yourself that in the nondiscriminatory expression of anger you are violating a physical as well as a spiritual law. Knowing we are taking years off our expected life span is sometimes challenge enough, because all of us prize life.

4. Cultivate a cheerful state of mind. Proverbs 17:22 says, "A cheerful heart does good like medicine . . . " Don't brood over wrongs as unpleasant situations, whether they are real or imagined.

5. Check the worry habit. Deliberately sing or play a record. Laugh and shout aloud, "I will not worry, for the Bible says, 'Nothing can hurt me'" (see Luke 10:19). Change your voice from one of a dismal drone to one that has an upward lilt. If you will go through the outward motions of the feelings you are wishing to

cultivate, you'll find your inner attitudes will change to correspond with your outward overt behavior.

Check the "disinterested in life" attitude. Start a project that will take you a while to finish, one which demands concentration, faith, and work. Then see it through! You'll find yourself facing each day with a refreshed outlook.

6. Discover something good in all that happens. "And we know that all that happens to us is working for our good if we love God and are fitting into his plans" (Rom. 8:28). Everything has a benevolent purpose and if you truly believe this, you never feel victimized by anything.

7. Deliberately single out a virtue in everyone with whom you have contact. No one is all bad. "Bad" behavior is only a display of the "good" in reverse. "Love thinks no evil (1 Corinthians 13:5 *KJV*) so make your mind think—and your lips say—something good about the other person.

8. Watch what you read and view on television. So much of the news is gloomy and disheartening. Often evil is lauded and virtue is blamed. Remember the adage, "If you glance at God and gaze at evil, you will be a pessimist. If you gaze at God and glance at evil, you will be an optimist."

9. Let the past go. It is dead time. It no longer exists and only memory keeps it alive. Refer to the pleasant happenings in your life. Write your successes down, if necessary, but live in the ever-present NOW. Antici-pate good tomorrows. Say, "I wonder what good will come to me today?" as your eyes open in the morning.

Don't muse on gloomy prophecies. Proclaim, "God is in all my tomorrows and I have no fears."

The Lord really encourages me when I read, in Isaiah 51:1-3, "Listen to me, all who hope for deliverance, who seek the Lord! Consider the . . . rock from which you were cut! . . . You worry at being so small and few, but Abraham was only one when I called him. But when I blessed him, he became a great nation. And the Lord will bless Israel again . . . Joy and gladness will be found there, thanksgiving and lovely songs."

Most of our worry is over things we think might happen and which don't exist.

10. Seek cheerful people for your companionship. Some people actually (whether consciously or unconsciously) have decided to be miserable. They find their identity by encompassing misery, and the symptoms of their "misery" disease are contagious. Seek happier people. If you are locked in with a miserable person, then innoculate yourself by refusing to respond to their disposition in a negative way. Your cheerfulness is contagious too.

11. Decide on one positive Scripture reference to sustain and hang your mind on all day. Repeat that passage when you feel irritability is creeping in upon you. The truth of God's Word is only revealed to you when it is acted upon and used. Repeat the Scripture, aloud if necessary, in the face of approaching melancholy.

12. At the close of the day, reflect upon your progress. Don't be afraid to bring your irritability up for judgment. If we deny it, we only hide its existence from

ourselves and live in self-deception. Face your irritability problem head-on and deal with it as you should do all sins of attitude or conduct.

13. Guard from inflicting another with your melancholic attitude or irritability. That person deserves to be happy, and you deserve self-respect. Some people may even take pleasure in your weakness, so why give them the opportunity?

14. Avoid self-pity. If you indulge in self-pity, your cause is lost. Don't baby your sins, your nerves, your irritation. Treat them as intruders. Be honest with yourself and your objective. Look at yourself, as an outsider might, and say, "You have no right to feel sorry for yourself. Get up and get going!"

15. Insist that happiness is your right. You have a right to be cheerful and contented. It is possible for you to live without displaying an irritable frame of mind. Avoid the temptation of sarcasm, the cool look, the cowardly backbiting, the hot tongue, the poison finger. It rots your soul. It ruins your day. It wrecks your health and shortens your life.

You deserve to be happy!

15. THE TRUTH SETS US FREE

Just how can we be free from anger? How can we be delivered from *any* negative emotion?

I received the following letter from a Christian friend who was struggling with feelings of pent up anger. If we will look at her experiences, we will discover some concepts which can assist each of us to conquer negative emotions and thereby be set free by the Truth.

Dear Ruth Ann,

I wanted to share with you a victory the Lord has given me over anger. I had always related anger only to a bad temper, but, I have found it is just one form of anger.

As you know, my mother passed away a few years ago. My father, who is in very poor health, came to visit me every day. He had a critical disposition and was depressed. The more I prayed for the Lord to keep him away, the more he came to see me. Finally, I became desperate and I wrote to you.

You remember you had me write three releases: to release, to the Lord, my possessive hold on the problems of other people. The first release was written to release my mother to the enjoyments of heaven. This brought immediate victory. Secondly, I wrote a release for my dad. This release didn't come right away. After each of his visits, you told me to go to my bedroom and pray, "I release him to you, Lord." I read and re-read the release you asked me to write. The word which stood out to me was "forgive." I couldn't release my father because I couldn't forgive him for his persistent negativism.

So after each of his visits, I began to say, "I forgive him and I release him to you, Lord." When I put release and forgiveness together, it worked. Peace came to my heart and it really felt good. In time my father began to change. He developed a closer walk with the Lord and was even enjoyable to be around. The Lord showed me that my dad was not all bad like I had thought. I was able to see and admire many of his good qualities.

Because of this tremendous victory, I began releasing many other people in my life. Most of the time I had to forgive before I could get results. The more I forgave and released, the cleaner and purer I felt on the inside.

The Lord showed me another sore spot in my life. I harbored resentment and bitterness toward my husband. He, like my father, was hot tempered and an expert at making cutting remarks. I responded by pouting and self-pity. I was capable of striking back with my mouth, but very seldom did. I didn't want to reap the guilt of scarring him that way with cutting words. Outwardly, nothing seemed to bother me, but inwardly I was very angry and bitter. It was an effort to show love toward him. Finally, through continued forgiveness and release, the Lord brought forgiveness in this area also. Every time anger stirred up inside me, I would ask the Lord to forgive me and I would have to forgive my husband. I was being cleansed of this pent-up anger.

This was the beginning of a healing in our marriage. I did not have a lot of builtup resentments, so love for my husband began to flow freely. The Lord was now free to begin working on the anger present in my husband. My husband would display anger, then feel guilty about the outburst, which in turn made him angrier. It was a vicious cycle. He had to learn to ask the Lord's forgiveness for each outburst of anger, then forget it.

My husband is a softball player and his victory

over anger was especially evident there. He had been known as the hothead of the team. Now he still has a big mouth, but he usually uses it for good to inspire and lift the rest of the team. With both of us having anger under control, true communication has opened up between us.

Freedom from anger has affected other areas of my life. I had fought a weight problem for years and could never gain complete victory over it. I could lose a few pounds for a few weeks, but I would then gain them, and more, back. After my victory over anger, I was able, through the Holy Spirit, to exercise self-control and lose this excess weight. It seems once you have exercised self-control in one area, other areas come easier. It took stubborn determination, but what was once impossible, became possible.

The Lord also gave me the inspiration plus the financial means to improve my personal appearance. I was able to look at myself in the mirror and say, "Hey, I love you and I like you," and "Boy, you sure look nice." It seemed when I accepted and loved myself, loving and accepting others just came naturally.

Another benefit of this victory is answers to prayers. The Lord is giving me many of the desires of my heart.

Looking back, all I can say, is, "Thank you Lord, for deliverance from anger."

Love, Rita.

This "freedom principle" worked for Rita in attaining freedom from anger. You, too, can be delivered from any negative emotion by the same freedom principle.

No victories are permanent without the ingredients which are contained in this letter from Rita. Let's look at four ingredients of her freedom-from-anger victory.

1. *Honesty.* Many of us pretend we have no problem because of false pride. There is no use to pretend we are functioning perfectly if we're not. Pretending a cancerous condition doesn't exist doesn't take it away. Pretense only gives the disease a chance to spread to every area until the whole person is affected. So it is with our spirits.

2. *Release and forgiveness.* The biggest key which turned the tide to deliverance (for Rita) was release and forgiveness. It's an age-old law of Christ, brought up-to-date and applied: "But when you are praying, first forgive anyone you are holding a grudge against . . ." (Mark 11:25). If we truly forgive people, we release them with no strings attached. When they are freed of our negative resistance toward them, we are freed. Both persons feel the freedom. We don't stand around to see the result of their wrongdoing.

3. *Admiration and approval* of others are like the blasts of a rocket. The powerful effect is that desire is kindled to receive the loving words coming toward them so their actions change.

4. *Self-love and forgiveness.* If we are to maintain our victories, we must be forgiving and approving of ourselves. The Lord's command is to love our neighbor *as* ourselves for we are an expression of Him. Whatever pent up negative emotions plague us, there is healing. "Would you like to get well?" Jesus asks (John 5:6).

16. YOU ASKED FOR IT—YOU'VE GOT IT!

"Why did I come?" I wondered as I glanced around at nearly 200 faces. I only recognized one person and he was in charge of the meeting. I had come 500 miles to attend a spiritual retreat. I remembered that "he who travels far to find that which he does not carry finds his sad heart still" (Emerson). A portable Christ goes with me wherever I go, but right then it would have felt nice to know somebody else who carried a portable Christ.

Deciding it was silly to stand around waiting, when probably dozens of others were thinking the same thing, I moved to a table where three girls from Newport, Virginia were chatting. I asked to sit down. One was a gracious, mature Christian who emanated poise and self-confidence. Another was a new Christian, getting used to her new saddle. She had been converted just a short while and still referred to her B.C. days. She was not uncomfortable because her companions were genuine and allowed her to be herself at her level of communication. The other traveler was Jane. All three young women possessed a particular charisma, but my affinity seemed to be with Jane.

Jane was a sweet, plain, girl. Her appearance wouldn't have distinguished her in the crowd, but she was open, honest, extremely intelligent and seeking. Her career was teaching English and drama in a Christian school.

It didn't take long to sense Jane was like multitudes of other believers who are hemmed in with LAW. At 27 years of age, she still hadn't found her identity. Many buried dreams seemed out of reach. In between each conference session, Jane and I had a private session of our own. As we shared, Jane began to shed layers of lack—feeling of inferiority and low self-esteem—like old skins.

"Is it okay to think well of myself?"

"Is it all right to fix myself up more attractively? Would I be humble and Christlike if I did?"

"What about all the sad Christians?"

"What will happen if I just cut loose and be me?"

"Would it be wrong to think, pray and plan big for my life?"

"I don't even think enough of myself to fix a good meal. I lean over the kitchen counter and eat whatever is convenient because I live alone."

"I wonder if there's a man in my life. I'd sure like to share my life with someone."

So our little sessions, outside the big sessions, were becoming the most precious times for us.

The Scriptures which teach us about the abundant life in Christ bring shafts of light. We just think it's too good to be true!

"Since He did not spare even his own Son for us but gave him up for us all, won't he also surely give us everything else?" (Rom. 8:32).

"All things are yours" (1 Cor. 3:21, *KJV*).

"Be delighted with the Lord. Then He will give you all your heart's desires" (Psa. 37:4).

"He tell us everything over and over again, a line at a time and in such simple words!" (Isa. 28:10).

As the concepts poured forth, our countenances were altered. The truth in Jane leaped with the truth in me, as the baby John leaped in the womb of Elizabeth, when Mary—with child—saluted her.

Before leaving the retreat, Jane and I found a quiet place to pray. "Deep called unto deep," and our souls were fused together forever. A part of each was in the other, and we were in the whole as sisters in Christ.

With joy I received these letters from Jane, a few days later:

Letter No. 1

Dear Ruth Ann,

Writing this note has been on my heart all week because I have much to share. The week has really been beautiful! I returned with a completely different outlook; I wasn't the same! I'm still praising God like I would never have dreamed. Something happened, Ruth Ann, something happened! I love everybody!

I'm trying to practice some of the suggestions I acquired there, especially the 'proper diet' suggestion. Preparing meals is the hardest because my time is so wrapped up in other things. But today I did some extra special preparation in planning and I'm looking forward to next week's meals. I've also made myself sit at the table with a complete table setting for the Lord. I was impressed. I don't know how it affected everyone else. I'm entertaining Monday; there isn't much time. Because of my schedule, I have to prepare the meal the previous day, but mentally I have something to look forward to. That's great!

I have deeply appreciated you and the book you gave me. I feel so free not playing those mental games with myself. I love me, inwardly and outwardly. I've taken special time to dress as attractively as I am able. I don't feel guilty about jewelry, clothes, etc., because I realize, because of your guidance, that I am the Jane form of Jesus and my choices reflect a different side of God's personality from anyone else's. Praise God.

Love, Jane

Letter No. 2

Dear Ruth Ann,

I haven't forgotten you, or your ministry! I have your book here near my "throne" and daily I eat off its goodness. I have thought about you so much. The school year has been exceptionally busy. I've rebelled at its busyness, too, which only puts me behind in His work.

The areas in which God is dealing with me are in the management of my time and management of a balanced diet. I've taken the weekend to plan my prayer time, my lessons through the end of the year, my daily and weekly routine, and I feel great. I never realized what planning and lists can do for our bodies. Such freedom I have! My eating habits have improved but I want to carefully plan a balanced diet. I am having headaches regularly! No stomach problems, however, praise the Lord. I like healing rather than pills.

God has brought into my life a very sweet guy! His likes are similar to mine and one of his hobbies is stage lighting. He has great acting abilities and enjoys theatre. The one thing which really makes me respect him, however, is his knowledge and practice of the Word. His desire is to work with juvenile delinquents. His concern is for the seventh, eighth and ninth grade levels (which is mine). He is presently working at a home for the mentally retarded, which is good for several reasons; one, it's excellent training (and polishing) and two, he's not in the area during the week. He's about 1½ hours drive from here so I don't anticipate anything and I get lots of surprises.

The goal God has for our cast production at school, of this secular comedy, is to show His love: we must be united in God's love. Our cast goal is unity as a family. It's not easy to be unified when so many are on different spiritual levels; some not in fellowship at all.

I love you. I think of you daily. Keep me in your prayers as you are in mine.

Lovingly,

Jane.

Letter No. 3 was a wedding invitation:

"We invite you to share in the celebration of our union in Christ in Norfolk, Virginia, July 16."

The wedding invitation represented a beginning of dreams, goals, freedom and abundance. It brought a breath of joy to my heart. Once again God had proven you can't dream, plan, or hope too much. He invites us to take off the grave clothes and stop acting poorly with our heavenly Father. "For it gives your Father great happiness to give you the Kingdom" (Luke 12:32). Ask Him for fullness of joy—and receive it. You'll get it!

17. FORGIVENESS: WHAT GREATER THERAPY?

You have heard it said that nature abhors a vacuum. Much of the good we want manifested in our lives cannot take place until we are rid of the old. If a person wants to be filled with God's Spirit, he seeks to be emptied of himself.

No one really knows what took place during the ten-day waiting period in the Upper Room, but the Bible says that when they were of one accord, the Holy Spirit came (see Acts 2:1-4). It must have taken some adjustment to bring opinionated Peter into alignment with others of equally strong prejudices.

It is usually when hearts are humbled and broken, that the Holy Spirit rushes in to fill the vacuum.

Jesus conditioned the forgiveness of our personal sins according to our forgiveness of those who have sinned against us.

Many people cannot advance in life or spiritual understanding because they are not getting rid of what they don't want or need. They need to create a vacuum. New life or creative thoughts do not flow easily in a cluttered situation.

One psychiatrist has said that the worst thing an alcoholic can do after receiving hospital treatment is to move back to a cluttered house. The exterior clutter adds to the inner confusion.

If you desire greater good in your life, what are you letting go of to make room for it? Letting go of the *lesser*, automatically makes room for the *greater*.

A prominent Christian man shared a resentment for someone who had lied about his daughter. Though urged by Christian friends to release his resentment, he was still unwilling. Within a few weeks, he suffered a heart attack. One morning, as he was listening to the radio by his bedside, a minister was reading from Matt. 6:14, 15. "Your heavenly Father will forgive you if you forgive those who sin against you; but if you refuse to forgive them, he will not forgive you." He asked the Lord for forgiveness and said, "God, I release those people of all the hurt they have incurred in my daughter's life."

In a few days, this father was well, active, and enjoying good health. He related his healing to his willingness to forgive.

We often think of forgiveness as being necessary when some very obvious transgression has occurred. But how do you check up on more ordinary sins? "How do I know I haven't forgiven someone?" you ask. Let your mind relax. Allow your memory to bring anyone across your mind out of the past or present. Think of your mind as if attached to an electroencephalogram. If no one crosses the indicator of your mind with eruption, you'll know there's nothing to release. But, if there's a lingering of some hurt which refuses to pass, you have some releasing to do.

I often allow God to bring anyone, past or present, to my mind. One day, there were two people my mind couldn't set free. I began to say several times, "I fully and freely forgive (John Smith). So far as I'm concerned the strain between us is finished forever. I wish him only good in his life and much blessing. I free him and let him go."

I found this act of release was simpler than I had imagined.

There was another eruption on the screen of my mind as I thought of another person. Case No. 2 took a little more effort, but I continued until I experienced a free-flowing, happy, loving thought about the person.

What feeling do you need to release?

Who are you locking in with an unforgiving spirit?
Who do you secretly wish to fail?

It could be the unnamed door that had kept you from
the good waiting to rush in upon you. Your own peace
of mind and health of soul are totally dependent upon
the relationship you establish in your world out there.
You can't afford *not* to be loving.

Forgiveness is the best possible umbrella for the
protection and promises of God. In refusing to forgive,
we bind ourselves to the law of jugment which tightens
a restricting band on us. It keeps out all consciousness of
God's constancy of blessing. You deserve to be
forgiving. Forgiving others is the best therapy we can
provide to enhance our spiritual health.

Prayer:
"Dear God, I fully and freely forgive the persons who
come to my mind. I completely loose them and let them
go. So far as I am concerned, they are free forever. I
pray you will bless them in every way. Thank you,
Lord. I am free too. Amen."

18. CHECK OUT YOUR JOYS

Without a doubt the basic desire of all us is to be
happy. Recently I asked a women's Christian fellowship
group: "What gives you a lift?"

I got some of the answers I had expected: a new
hairdo, getting my bills paid, helping another person,
buying a new dress, changing the furniture. I had to
agree. All of these things give me a lift, too.

My next question was: "What would it take to make you happy?"

- "I'd be happy if my husband was saved."
- "I want my whole family in church."
- ". . . harmony in my home."
- ". . . my parents converted."
- ". . . a new house."
- ". . . my husband to come back home."

Then I asked, "Could you be happy without it?"

The apostle Paul learned to be abased and how to abound. In either state he had learned to be content. "I have learned how to get along happily whether I have much or little . . . I have learned the secret of contentment in every situation . . . for I can do everything God asks me to with the help of Christ who gives me the strength and power" (Phil. 4:11-13).

Joys in tangible things are dangerous.

Joys dependent on loved ones and people alone are threatened joys.

A missionary family from Calcutta lost six children in a landslide. One child lived long enough to tell how the oldest child had gathered the siblings together and said, "Jesus is coming for us. Let's pray."

The parents did not try to explain the purpose or reason for this tragedy. Instead, they used it. They started an orphanage to house 350 children without homes or parents. The mother who lost her children in the landslide said, "I never had a sorrow." Her sorrow became her song.

Joys riveted in tangible things or people are subject to a moment's change. No man is safe unless he can use anything and everything that happens to him. If anyone kicks you, make him kick you toward the goal. Make evil serve you! Jesus did this at Calvary.

No man can take your good from you. A great soul once said, "What can death do to me, for I've already died?" Galatians 2:20 tell us that we've already been to our own funeral and come back again with Christ living within us.

Several years ago, mission leaders in Haiti asked us to come spend three weeks with them during their mid-winter camp. I had never been on a large plane, nor even out of the country, and I was carried away with excitement. My emotions were clear out of hand. We had been called to minister, and I was hung up with a plane ride and palm trees! In that shape, I knew that I couldn't relate except on a human level. So I went to prayer, and asked God to remove the human joys from my heart in order that all I experienced was His joy. His joy is the only joy I feel permanently safe with.

I felt a surge of power and strength for the task. My husband and I became spiritual soldiers, going to battle, and we experienced a mighty moving of the Spirit during our stay in Haiti. Our joys were in the Lord and were abounding.

When our first trip to the Holy Land was being planned, I got emotionally excited again! The fact that I would walk where Jesus walked was just too much for me to handle. Once again, I got alone with God and offered up my joy for His joy. I was safe with His joy and had a glorious time.

The principle of checking our our joys was never stronger than when our daughter was born.

Our firstborn was a boy. We called him by his name seven months before his birth. I wasn't sure before the second child. We wanted a girl, but didn't ask the Lord for any special favors.

I heard the news in the delivery room—that we had a *girl*—and I was so elated! In fact, I laid awake all night bursting with happiness. We had a girl! Sometime in the early hours, however, the Lord reminded me, "Where are your joys?"

I felt like Abraham. Did I love Him or my "Isaac"? I didn't want to have to prove my love, like Abraham, so I hastened to answer, "Lord, you are my joy. You always will be. I offer up the joys of my new baby to you."

The next morning my husband, Don, was at the door of the hospital room. He told me how he had risen at 5:00. He saw my clothes littered about, reminding him of my hurried departure for the hospital, and he was overcome with our new joy.

As he sat down to read the Word, Don read Psalm 73:25, "Whom have I in heaven but you? And I desire no one on earth as much as you!"

Without our being together, God had checked each of our earthly attachments, and we had surrendered the joy of our new baby.

Abraham gave Isaac back, twice blessed. Nothing is safe until it's offered. Isaac was no longer threatened.

Have you checked your joys lately? Are they based on tangible things that are as a vanishing vapor?

Do you cling to loved ones as your source of happiness? Are you postponing joy until the perfect situation?

Take a step of surrender today. Offer up the tangibles of your sources of joy.

Tell God all your springs are in Him. "All to Jesus I surrender. I surrender all." Here are my joys, Lord!

19. RELEASE YOUR WRINKLED APPLES

A few summers ago we experienced a delightful wedding. Our only daughter, Ann Victoria, was married to a beautiful young man from Santa Rosa, California named Rick Lund. It seems like the summer was one long wedding. Those of you that have lived through such an experience can envision all the details and preparation involved, not to mention the financing of the big event.

The wedding night was a beautiful climax to many hours of planning, sharing, hoping, dreaming and a lifetime of praying. Perhaps it was all the pre-praying that made the time so blessed. The expected tears never came. I came with my crying gear, a big white hankie, and the groom's mother carried a package of Kleenex. She used hers, but I came home with a dry handkerchief.

The Christmas before the wedding, Rick came to Iowa to ask Ann's dad for permission to marry her. We trusted Ann's mature judgment, and during his three week stay we felt the beginnings of a very special attachment to him. His own father had died when Rick was ten, and a natural father-son relationship sprang up between my husband and the wonderful young man who was to become our daughter's husband.

The vacation went quickly by, and back went Ann and Rick to college, to finish out the year with excitement and planning. The wedding date was soon set for August 3. All agreed this would give time to plan, and time to work to accumulate some needed finances.

One day a letter arrived that said, "Mother and Dad, Rick is going to work at home in Santa Rosa this summer and I'm going to stay near his home with his sister. I'll work, save my money and come out a couple weeks early to plan for the wedding."

Well, Ann's idea didn't particularly thrill us, so we went into our family huddle. This time Father dictated the letter.

"Ann, we believe since you still have a home to come to, you should come here for the summer to work and prepare for your wedding."

A response was soon to come: "Mother and Dad, Rick and I read and reread your letter. We know your mature judgment is best and Rick and I will be home May 8th."

Now, that put a new kink in our minds! We not only had one, but two people heading toward Iowa to spend three months before the wedding.

Since Rick and Ann accepted our mature judgment, there was nothing to do but make plans for two instead of one. A very wonderful home opened up to him, but Rick found many logical reasons for being at our house most of the time; and so we found most of our nicely managed routine soon upset with two lovers.

We certainly learned a lot of life's lessons from this

couple. After three days Rick got restless. All attempts at finding a job failed. He and Ann earnestly, and finally remembered a principle she had believed and used in her life as a teenager: "To have you must give." Without telling us, they combined his remaining $30 in the bank and her last $3; and put it in the Lord's work. Their secret and their faith brought immediate results. Our son telephoned and said, "Rick, go over to such-and-such company. They need someone for siding houses this summer." That day Rick had his job.

Meanwhile, Ann walked into the supermarket to buy some groceries. As she was checking out, the manager asked, "What are you doing this summer?"

Ann replied, "Looking for a job."

"How would you like to work here as cashier?"

"I'd love it," she said. The grocery store was located 2½ blocks from our house.

That summer we watched those young people pray over every detail of their needs, and saw God supply those needs. Rick needed both some white and some cream-colored pants. He had looked for some time but hadn't been able to find his size. After they described to the Lord *exactly* what they wanted, they walked into one men's department store and found precisely what they had requested. Both pairs of pants were hanging side by side on the clothing rack.

Our schedule was already full, and with two newcomers in our household it soon got fuller. Have you ever experienced the amount of laundry young collegians can stack up? I felt like praying a special blessing on my washer so it would hold up for the summer.

Laundry, however, wasn't the only surprise. The big change for me was cooking! My husband and I are diet-watchers. Rick, we soon discovered, must eat volumes of food to just break even. He's naturally thin so he needs extra weight! Extra weight means extra food!

Our simple rations changed to bulging food shelves and a constantly-visited, full refrigerator which kept opening like a revolving door.

I have a real dislike for wasting anything. For weeks there had been about five wrinkled apples in our refrigerator. On one of his trips to the refrigerator, I suggested Rick eat them. He said he didn't care for them right then. He thought they looked rather wrinkled.

One evening Rick was the only one eating. My husband was gone, Ann was working, I was dieting. As I planned the menu I spied my wrinkled apples. I thought it was just the appropriate time to make proper use of them as a salad. I felt fairly safe in the assumption that if I peeled off all the wrinkles Rick would eat those perfectly good apples and never know the difference.

I placed the meal on the table, satisfied it was tasty-looking. I felt especially good about the apples. Rick ate the whole meal and never touched the apples on the salad plate! I suggested several times that he eat his salad with his meal. After the meat and potatoes were all gone, the apples remained. I thought perhaps he had saved them for dessert.

Rick caught my eye at that point and said, "Aren't these those wrinkled apples?" When I nodded my head in assent, he said, "I really don't believe I care for any."

I mumbled something like, "We should eat everything

set before us with thanks and not ask questions," and whisked the apples into the garbage!

Those wrinkled apples were the first fly in the ointment to a lovely relationship. I knew if I allowed a root of resentment to begin I could have trouble for three months over less important things than apples. I fled to my bedroom and whipped out my pencil and wrote with determination, "Lord Jesus, I release Rick from not eating my apples. I love him. He is beautiful and he doesn't have to eat them. I am free now and he is free. Amen."

I came out smiling and sweetness reigned.

The summer progressed with an unbroken fellowship. Oh, how happy I am to know I can keep the channels of life free from hostile emotions. If I hadn't, I might have missed this letter:

> Dear Mom and Pop,
> We feel excited, but sad in a way, to be leaving. Living under the roof of such as yourselves is an experience that few people ever have. I've learned to genuinely love and respect you two in a way I've never experienced before. I truly love you two and I feel like a son, a very proud son. Thanks so much for yourselves, your commitment to God, and your daughter.
> Your son,
> Rick.

Why don't you release your wrinkled apples?

20. WORD POWER

Your *word* is your power. Your choice of words always do one of two things?: they build up or tear down. Every word discharged from your mouth produces results.

If we continually speak despairingly of our problems, we will probably live to "eat our own words." Talking about a problem "cements" the problem in our minds. Talking about sickness enhances the condition.

Repetition of any "word" fixes a connotation of that word in a person's mind and causes it to become a moving force to their body. How important it is to exercise the power of repeating good, wholesome, honest, pure, vivacious words!

The way I discovered the actual creative power of my own "words" was unique.

We had been having a series of prayer meetings in our church. There were two prayer meetings at noon on Mondays and Wednesdays; mid-week prayer on Thursday; a Friday night home prayer meeting; and a 6:00 prayer meeting on Sunday morning.

Now, allow me to state that I like prayer meetings! And I know nothing is done effectively without prayer; but I was exhausted trying to keep pace. Besides attending all those group prayer meetings, I still tried to maintain my personal time with God (even if that time ended up to be in the wee hours of the night. Because of these times of prayer, great things were happening! I didn't want to miss anything, but my body began to sag with fatigue.

One morning I opened by Bible to see if I could discover an answer for the sheer exhaustion I felt. My eyes fell on Joel 3:10, "Let the weak *say* I am strong" (*KJV*).

I decided I was *certainly weak*, and *the command was*

clear. I began to verbally assert, "I am strong." At first my very words seemed like mockery; but I persisted, and soon my whole body and spirit swung into harmony with what I was saying. I rose to the level of my audibilized decree of faith. I found myself soaring off to another prayer meeting with plenty of strength—and some to spare.

Recently I visited with a friend whom I hadn't seen for months. She had just been released from the psychiatric ward. The time I had to spend with her was short, but I hoped to make constructive use of our brief time together.

I was convinced I would help this woman if she would cooperate in reprogramming her thoughts and words. She was beautiful and had much to live for. It was unbearable to see her life being smothered.

The battle of words went something like this:

"You are so beautiful and have a tremendous potential."

"No, I'm really dumb because I quit school . . . My folks were so strict. That's why I'm in this shape . . . I'm filled with fear . . . I have deep, deep depressions . . . I have no friends . . . I've lost all interest in my home . . . My kids bore me . . . I'm tired of being surrounded by sad people . . . I wish I could die. If I could *only* have *one* happy day."

Every positive or approving statement was met with total despair. My friend was affirming her faith in the power of gloom. Our time together was soon spent, and I had to leave her. I realized the only way I could reach her on a prolonged basis would be through prayer.

One day I read Job 22:28, "You will also decree a

thing, and it will be established for you" (*NASB*). I took stock of my verbal assertions and discovered that unknowingly, in the routine chatter of the day, some of my words had become my prisons. If I say I can't do something, it's pretty certain that I can't.

Words can imprison us or set us free. We can develop an awareness of our "Word Power" by examining how often we use our "faith" or our "slave" vocabulary.

Our *Faith* vocabulary might include:

1. I like me.
2. I'll win.
3. I'll forgive.
4. I am loving.
5. I'm happy.
6. Positively.
7. I'll do it.
8. I believe.

Our *slave* vocabulary would be:

1. I'm a loser.
2. I was born that way.
3. I'm stupid.
4. I'm bored.
5. I'm afraid.
6. I'm weak.
7. I'm hopeless.
8. I hope so.
9. I can't.
10. It's my parent's fault.
11. I'm not ready yet.
12. At my age.

If a replay of our vocabulary used during any given day were made, we would know why 95% of us live in a depressive state of mind. Our thoughts and words of *lack* create a condition of a lack on every level of life.

We should look for the good in everything and everybody!

A precious family from our church are watching for

one good happening, each day, that they can share at the dinner table in the evening. They report that, at first, the children shared very general things—like recess, lunch time, etc. But one day their eight-year-old excitedly announced, "I'm the new squadron leader in my class!" The whole family gloated in his success and went out to buy a trophy with printed words, "The World's Best Squadron Leader."

On another occasion, the husband was excited because one of his ideas had been accepted at the office; and the mother stubbed her toe quite hard and said, "Praise the Lord, I had my shoe on."

The very salvation of our souls is accomplished not only by our heart's belief, but according to our spoken words. Faith cannot function without verbal cooperation. Faith is not real to a person until it has been voiced by their lips.

The apostle Paul writes, in Romans 10:8-10: "For salvation that comes from trusting Christ—which is what we preach—is already within easy reach of each of us; in fact, it is as near as our own hearts and mouths. For if you tell others with your own mouth that Jesus Christ is your Lord, and believe in your own heart that God has raised him from the dead, you will be saved. For it is by believing in his heart that a man becomes right with God; and with his mouth he tells others of his faith, confirming his salvation."

I vividly recall counseling with a woman who had just prayed to receive Christ. In doing so, she had fulfilled all the requirements to be saved, except one—belief.

I told her that her salvation was as near as her mouth. I pointed out to her how Paul had mentioned a person's confession of faith with their mouth even before believing with their heart. This happens because the heart automatically follows what the mouth verbalizes!

In a few moments this new Christian woman started verbalizing her salvation. Her heart responded with a spiritual witness, and she went soaring out of our meeting with unspeakable joy! She came back with a glowing testimony the next week. The longed-for manifestation of her salvation had been as near as her verbalization.

Your happiness could be as near as your mouth! You can create your own mood. The law of "verbalization" is established, but you must put it in operation by making righteous decrees.

Your bondage can be changed immediately by a positive declaration of your words. Your fears can be silenced by a positive declaration of peace.

You can often instantaneously free yourself and others by the power of your positive words.

. Decree you can. Decree you are able. Decree your financial needs are met. Decree you are confident.

The law of creative word power is backed by the God who has declared, "I will not take back one word of what I said" (Psa. 89:34).

Use your "Word Power." There can never be a limit to your influence of good—to yourself and to others—

and function in the spiritual freedoms of "Word Power."

Part III

Your Problems

Part III

21. HOW TO BE SECOND AND WIN

We had one evening to spend in Rome before coming home from our Holy Land venture. Night had fallen on the old city of Rome, its Vatican, its Colliseum and its Catacombs.

It was raining hard, although we weren't aware of it until we walked out the front door of the hotel. Rather than waste time, we left our umbrella in our suitcase upstairs.

Being a lifetime saver I thought we could save more money by riding the city bus. My husband reluctantly went along with my suggestion, but after eight unsuccessful attempts to get our Italian directions straight, even I wished we had gotten a taxi! However, we finally dragged our dripping bodies onto a city bus.

Everyone wore dark blue, black or gray. Four girls, sitting across the aisle from one another, talked loudly and laughed uproariously, much to the embarrassment of all. But at least their noise provided a break in that dark, somber picture. The faces of the passengers matched the darkness. I thought about the 39 percent voting Communists at the polls, and wondered what more that party would do to darken the lives of these people.

The once proud Rome could only boast of its past. But so much of its past was shameful. Crimes and sensuality had brought Rome's knees bending, from a world empire to a country with only a past.

But again, as in Jerusalem, I knew we were in a city of the future. The bus' tour guide talked freely of the city which sits on the seven hills in Revelation. It was not easy to imagine both the future and fall of Rome.

My husband and I got off our city bus to do some shopping. After 1½ hours of shopping, two drenched people hailed a taxi.

If you're not ready for heaven, riding in downtown Rome about 6:30 p.m. is not the thing to do. There is no sensible, logical reason why those thousands of little cars, driving without rhyme or reason, shouldn't be hitting each other. I decided I was better off with my eyes shut.

As we whirled around the Spanish steps, with hundreds of cars missing us by a hair, we nosed right into another taxi driver. Both vehicles came to an abrupt halt and waited for the other to move. Neither one did. The traffic just went around and dodged in and out, criss-crossing in every fashion. No policeman would risk his life directing traffic, so everyone was left at the mercy of each other.

Neither taxi driver was one bit merciful. Pretty soon the fists were shaking and each driver stubbornly refused to move. Finally the other driver wrenched his car sideways and whirled around us. I felt relieved until I saw he had stopped right behind us.

You'd have thought our driver would be satisfied just to be on his way, but not so. He had to stick his head out of the window and call a few obsenities to the other driver, now out of his car. When this display of anger didn't provide enough revenge, our driver jumped from the car and charged up to the other man, shouting loudly. I was glad at that point I couldn't understand any Italian. Some words were just too close to miss.

By this time my husband had jumped from the back seat. I thought he was going to separate the drivers, so I added my encouraging shouts to the confusion. Meanwhile, the traffic continued to lunge around our driver and his colleague. The two cars were still stalled impudently in the wild traffic. Finally, our shaking driver got back in the car. My husband returned to my side, and I thought, "Praise the Lord, we're on our way!" But my relief was short-lived! The other driver, suddenly overcome with a fresh burst of anger, rushed up to our car window and stuck his fist in the open window, muttering threats and looking horribly fierce. Whether it was my "Oh God, help!" or not, that did it! They tore themselves loose from sweet revenge and away we went. Our driver kept talking to us and to himself as we sped through the streets. We couldn't understand his Italian, so we just grunted now and then.

I wondered at the savage beast within people which refuses to lend another the right-of-way.

It's as old as Cain and Abel. Anger is murder in a mild form.

It would be nice if being a Christian solved all these self-vindication problems, but very often the believer coils like a serpent when his rights are tread upon.

Jesus told us what to do about our anger, but

knowing what to do and applying it in a crisis is the trick.

A man must be so much in tune with God every day that it becomes harder for him to move from his center of tranquility than to stay within it.

If we live with an idea of separateness we will never surrender our cloak to the man who takes our coat.

If we have not practiced denying ourselves of the luxury of self-defense in our daily habit, we'll never go the second mile when we are asked to go one.

I haven't had to turn my rosy cheek to the other side after being slapped, but I have learned to suffer in silence when railed upon. I have learned to refuse to enter into a cause where I knew I had been harshly judged, refusing my right to set it straight.

The psalmist says, "Your (God's) gentleness has made me great" (Psa. 18:35). A gentle person is a powerful person. A man who controls his spirit is greater than he who takes a city.

Anger poisons the blood, causes a malfunctioning of the body processes and dissipates our strength.

Some individuals would rather be right than to save their home or to save a child. Their harsh demands and brittle spirits have closed the door on love which once burned brightly in their heart. Divorce is often easier than an apology. A continual warfare is often chosen instead of three magic words: "I am sorry," or, "I am wrong."

Jesus had an answer for everything. He not only had the answer. He was the answer! It is that we no longer live but He within us (see Gal. 2:20). Or as E. Stanley

Jones said it, "I've come back from my own funeral and I'm alive in the Alive."

We won't have to have second thoughts about how to react but our first thought shall be: "After you." "Be my guest." "May I help you?" "You first." "Take my seat." "You can have it."

Right now some of you could change a portable hell into a portable heaven by writing a letter to someone whose very name causes you to stir with resentment. A telephone call could raise you from the human to the divine.

The child you apologize to can look at you with new respect and honor.

When we're in Rome, let's not do as Romans do. When we're in the Rome of our own small city, let's remember the words of our Lord, "In honor preferring one another" (Rom. 12:10, *KJV*). Say it a hundred times a day, and restrict every negative in your life, if you want to break through to a new and blessed relationship with the Roman citizens in your life.

22. ALIVE TO GOD!

I guess everyone has a few mental gymnastics they use to get them over a situation they fear.

I was scheduled to sing for a large gathering recently; and while I'm not afraid to sing in a small group or to solo while I play the piano at home, it annoys and condemns me that I fear to sing on other occasions. Why should I fear at all when the Bible says, in 1 John

4:18, "Perfect love casts out fear" (*KJV*). Phillips' translation of the same verse reads: "Fully developed love expels every particle of fear." So, why should I fear anything? Perfect love is a perfect consciousness of God at all times.

Why should I respond with fear when I lose my billfold? Must I allow my blood pressure to soar and hot flashes of fear to take over?

Why should I fear a cold, a draft, a headache, a trip to the dentist or a tetanus shot, if "perfect love casts out fear"?

Why do we fear our children's walk to school, their unhappiness in the nursery, or fear they won't be accepted by their peers?

Must we have that new chair, that new dress? Must we take the trip or attend the party? Should possessing or not possessing material goods really disturb us?

Why should we tremble at the news in the newspaper and worry over the economy?

Should we feel badly when we want someone we think is special to like us, and they don't seem to know we're there?

Should our self-image crumple when we're not invited to the fellowship meeting when others are?

When we make one thing, one person, or persons more important than others, we descend to the level of stage fright, fear, rejection and worry. We are inwardly paralyzed. Since the "inward" becomes the "outmost," we function awkwardly.

Jesus said, "Be anxious for nothing" (Phil. 4:6 *NASB*), so why are we anxious?

I am in the process of learning to take the importance out of happenings, people and circumstances.

Colossians 3:3 says, "You should have as little desire for this world as a dead person does. Your real life is in heaven with Christ and God."

The biggest trick for the believer is to know he really is dead: dead to worry; dead to blame or praise; dead to fear; dead to defeat; dead to doubt; dead to negativism and lack.

Romans 6:11 says, "So look upon your old sin nature as dead and unresponsive to sin, and instead be alive to God, alert to him, through Jesus Christ our Lord." When I respond to the negative forces of life, I have acknowledged that I am alive to sin. At that moment, I don't know who I am. When I don't know who I am, I react to a crisis. I become threatened by a thousand life situations which are subject to change in a moment.

If I am totally alive unto God, all the exaggerated negatives which plague my mind and make me abnormal as a Christian, begin to shrivel and disintegrate.

Special incidents and special people are then robbed of their importance. All of life is one big important adventure, lived by the power of God surging through me with fearless energy. I can plunge into life with enthusiasm, without being threatened, because my life is not held together by fragments or isolated experiences; but it is a fusion into God which gives me wholeness. Will I allow myself to be made whole?

If I lose my billfold, I can say, "it's unimportant for my Father is rich. It is His billfold. If He wants me to have His billfold, He'll bring it back to me. It's unimportant."

"The suitcase which was lost at the airport didn't

arrive in time for the conventions. It doesn't matter! It's unimportant."

"I might get sick. If so, the disease will probably turn around when they find out who I am. (a believer in whom Christ resides). If not, if He wants arthritis in His arm, that's His problem."

When there are people we hope will like us, and they don't seem to have noticed our presence, it's all right, because we are Spirit-filled people. We don't need to obstruct that relationship by seeking to know them in a "special way," in our human personalities.

If someone very dear rejects me, I won't like it! But I can transfer it to my "unimportant file." I know that if they knew me, they'd like me, because their mask is no different than mine. I can be myself because I am not suspicious of myself. I know *myself* is really *Himself*.

I no longer need fear being vulnerable. It's all right for me to admit "I don't know," "I am sorry," or "I am wrong." Now I don't have to keep up a false pretense. I don't fear being found out, for it's unimportant if they know my weakness.

I need not fear tomorrow because "each day has enough trouble of its own" (Matt. 6:34, *NASB*). God is in all my tomorrows so why should I stay awake and worry. He's already promised not to go to sleep, so why shouldn't I get my sleep?

If I am not invited to the "beautiful people" fellowship, I can "drink the cup" with the Lord of the universe. We can travel together to any place in the world together in a split second for our fused spirits know no limits. The party is unimportant.

If I missed a measure in the organ solo on Sunday

morning it's unimportant. One hundred years from now, it will make no difference.

The lost suitcase is the Lord's. If He wants to bring it back when I pray, I'll use it for Him. If not, I'll wash the neck of the dress I'm wearing.

I don't need to say, "It's my chair. It's my house. It's my car." I will use all the things afforded to me generously, and not demonstrate over the plenty, for He has told me, "All things are yours." I know whatever I need will always be there, so I don't need to own my house or my bank account. I can simply use it for awhile and then keep it circulating in the world's supply. I can hold it loosely, with a twinkle in my eye, because I might need to leave it in a hurry.

My children are His possession, so I don't have to nervously chart their course. My husband is God's boy, so I can allow God to direct "His boy" in an atmosphere of love and approval. It's unimportant if present appearances lie to me and tell me otherwise because I know the truth. I can judge righteous judgment (from God's standpoint). I know that ceaseless prayer means instant ability to say in every crisis of life, "All is well." As my words, so shall it be.

So if I'm to sing for 2 or 2,000, it's unimportant.

The glory of the mystery is, "to live is Christ." With every increasing year, we can say, "The best is yet to come." The Bible says, "it doth not appear what we shall be," *Now,* and in the ages to come. (I John 3:2 *KJV*). Even death cannot hurt us because we're already dead (see Col. 3:3). Life cannot hurt us either. "Neither death, nor life, nor angels, nor principalities, nor powers, nor things present, nor things to come, nor

height, nor depth, nor any other creature shall be able
to separate us from the love of God . . . (Rom. 8:38, 39
KJV).

So, come learn along with me. *There's nothing
important, but being alive to God.*

23. "SHE PROMOTED ME"

My husband and I recently returned from a retreat for
pastors and physicians.

One of the first lectures was given by a psychologist
from Tampa, Florida. He began his series by telling
some of his life story.

He is now a Jewish Christian. He was in Germany at
the height of the Jewish purge under Hitler. The names
of Jewish people destined for deportation were con-
spicuously posted in the city square. Our speaker was
kicked out of high school. His father lost his job, and
was soon taken to a concentration camp; never to be
heard of again.

The Germans put a lot of priority on those people
who worked with their hands so, the conference
speaker, became an apprentice to a locksmith, hoping
this would make him less offensive to the officers of
the German army who descended on them daily.

In pre-war days, the family had a Catholic house-
keeper who talked frequently to him about Jesus.
Though it had no apparent meaning to him then, it was
a contributing factor to his eventual turning to
Christ as his personal Messiah.

There was one definite loophole that helped protect
him from the Nazi purge, he told us. His mother was

American, and the Germans were apprehensive about exciting the Americans more than necessary over their treatment of the Jews.

Thus it was, that this Jewish youth was exchanged for a German prisoner held captive in the United States.

Upon landing in the U.S., he was given a New Testament. He joined the American armed forces and was severely wounded in battle. In fact, his leg was nearly shot off. The bits of flesh holding his leg together were full of shrapnel. He was put in the "hopeless ward" with many unfortunate soldiers like himself.

One morning, after lying lifeless for many days, he noticed a Red Cross lady making her way through the ward with candy and peanuts. She stopped at his bed, and after an exchange of words she said, "I believe your leg can be completely well. May I pray for you?"

Thinking it couldn't do any harm, he said yes.

"From the moment she said, 'I believe your leg can be completely well,' she set up an expectancy in me. She promoted me. Her words of faith and confidence, every day as she passed my bed, told me she saw something of importance in me that I didn't see in myself."

In two weeks he lifted his leg off the bed, and in a few more weeks he was out of bed, praying with the other "hopeless ward" patients. In a matter of time every man in that ward was released.

He said, "I learned to love Jesus through love encounters before I was aware of the certainty of the Personality."

It is definitely true: we trigger reactions in other people whether we are conscious of it or not.

When you see certain people, you feel certain ways.

If you're in a hospital and the doctor walks in, you feel better immediately, whether he has touched you or not.

If a nurse tells you it takes six weeks for your cure, you set your mind for six weeks. If another nurse says two weeks, you set your mind toward that duration of time.

A young convert was sharing, with dismay, his inability to cope with certain types of Christians. He said, "They bring out the worst in me. I feel like the old life tries to recapture me when I'm in their presence."

If a minister walks by your bedside while you are sick, you feel better.

If we go to church, we feel better.

We trigger reactions in people, because, we, or someone around us, has set up expectations.

I'm reminded of the conversation I had recently with a pastor's wife. She and her husband were providing us with a ride to the airport to catch a plane. Our husbands sat in front, and we chatted together in the back seat of the car. My friend told me about her longing for a definite ministry in their church. "I can do a lot of things a little bit," she said, "but nothing really well." Every time she spoke, she talked of her inadequacy; and, in doing so, she crippled the edge of her sprouting, creative hopes and dreams.

At one point in our conversation, I asked her if she were aware she was doing this. She replied, "Yes, I am becoming increasingly aware I have done this to myself."

This lovely Christian woman needed someone to promote her! She needed someone to grant her unconditional permission and approval to be the person she wanted to be, and to have the ministry she so desired. She needed to give her *own self* that permission by accepting herself.

Have you ever considered the possibility that some man, some woman, some business associate, some pastor, some child, is waiting for you to promote him.

You can start the vibrations of "expectation" in another life today, and my guess is that the person in need of your promotion is very near at hand.

Prayer:
"Father, show me today where I may promote others and also allow myself to grow. I want to set up an expectation of good things in another person's life. Amen."

24. "GET OUT OF MY SUN"

On our Holy Land trip, one of our side tours included Greece, the homeland of several of Paul's churches. After a tour of the Acropolus, Mars Hill, and Athens, we were ready to journey to Corinth the next day.

In Corinth, our guide told a story that made my coming take on a new profoundness.

Diogenes was a philosopher who enjoyed the riches of a simple life, she related. His life and teachings made him greatly sought after by the small and the great. His only earthly possessions were a barrel to hold water and a cup to put to his lips. One day while watching the birds drink water, he concluded if the birds didn't need a cup he didn't either. He threw away his cup and drank water from his hand.

One day the shadow of Alexander the Great, Emperor of the World, fell upon Corinth. He had heard of Diogenes and had come to honor him in any way he could.

"What, good Diogenes, can I do for you?"

Diogenes stretched his head sideways and said, "Please, sir, get out of my sun."

My mind was quickly jolted from my outer world to my inner world. The chilly weather suddenly seemed unimportant.

I felt like saying to my wandering thoughts while enroute to Corinth, "Get out of my sun." There are always Alexanders to obstruct our sun. I don't know what your Alexanders are. I don't always know for sure what mine are until some Diogenes jars me to attention. Would you dare to challenge a few of these Alexanders with me? Perhaps in so doing, the sun may shine more brightly on us both.

1. *The Alexander who wants to be courted.* This Alexander wants you to come out of the solitude of your spirit. He admires your poise, but he questions your secret. He wants your label out in the open so he can understand you. Once labeled, he can pick you apart. Once you have courted him and exposed your pearls, he shakes you off like any other beggar. He requests conformity. Once the mystery is gone, he goes on to another. Jesus trod the winepress alone. The soul has a sanctuary for itself and its Lover. Don't come out for the Alexanders who court you.

2. *The Alexanders who flash their badges.* They would get your attention by spiritual name dropping. Have you heard this one, or that? Have you been there? They remind you of their large institutions. In the presence of these Alexanders we quickly surrender. We are carried away with cheap affection. We conclude they're better than us because of who they know, where they've been, and the badge on their coats.

The way to discern true greatness is how I feel when this kind of strutting Alexander leaves my presence. Does his brand of goodness have an edge to it which makes me nobler? Does it make me feel there's a light shining in me also? Do I have a strange fire lit within me which makes me look up to God and say, "I could do that for you."

If not, it's not a doctrine of love and cannot be of God.

3. *The Alexander which wants to think for you.* He wants you to have a secondary testimony and, since his is the best, it must be accepted. He knows your duties better than you. He has heard God's voice in the night for you. He can only see you within certain limitations of his own idea for you. If that idea doesn't match his own, he will (figuratively) draw his sword and chop your head off. He can tell you where to live, how to look, what car is best, a likely salary for your kind. He can tell you how to pray and how not to pray. He knows the shibboleth of spiritual talk, and if it's the in thing to say or do, he'll believe you if you do it; if you don't, he won't.

It is easy to bow down to the Alexanders who would think for you. But to do so would be crime against the pilgrims, the catacomb dwellers, the Joan of Arc's, the prophets, the mystics and the Spirit of Christ Himself. To maintain a free spirit centralizes your force and joins you to the spirits of just men made perfect. It sharpens the impression on your own character.

Being noble means to be free.

So let us say to the Alexanders who:
1. Want to court us,
2. Flash their badges at us,
3. Want to think for us—
"'Get out of my sun.' I knew God before you came and I'll know God after you go."

25. TAKE CONTROL OF YOUR TIME

"I don't have time."

Time for what?

Time is life and it is irreplaceable. Jesus said to "make the best of your time despite all the difficulties of these days" (Eph. 5:6, *Phillips*). If you can master your time, you can control your life and make the most of it.

Even if you are a clock-watcher and gain the most from every moment, you could be very unfulfilled.

I lived on an apple farm as a child. Every fall we harvested and exported many truckloads of apples. This required thousands of boxes. That's right! I made boxes. I found I made a lot more boxes if I brought my radio out of the shop and turned it to the 15 minute programs. My goal was to make a box in a minute. In order to do this every pound had to count. I made more money, but it was a mechanical way to operate. A person chained to a clock can be a bore, but I did redeem the time.

We need to do some intelligent thinking about how we really want to use our time. Perhaps we could work less and enjoy life a lot more. Being effective is even more important than being efficient.

Barbara is the church receptionist. She's held that position for 14 years. Since I'm not too good at remembering, I tell Barb what I need to remember, and then go about my work. I know she will tell me when and what to do. She reminds me to go to the dentist and my husband to cut his hair. She orders our plane tickets and keeps our appointments in order. But, Barb is more than our organizer. She has helped us to enjoy our journey. Barb knows how to control our time for us.

Getting control of your time is not being super-organized or preoccupied with each moment. Life becomes a burden to such a person, and he's as bad off as the totally disorganized person.

A time-obsessed person is extremely concerned with detail. I hate to admit that I'm close to this obsession. Since I recognize my tendency, I'm trying to do something about it. I became aware that when I sat down to watch a TV show, I made sure I had some sewing in my hand, a pencil and paper nearby, and one or two books laying open to read intermittently. Needless to say, relaxing comes hard for me.

When my husband and I get a day to relax we are sometimes frustrated because we don't know how or what to do. In fact, Mondays (off) can be the most frustrating day of the week for a pastor who doesn't know how to relax. Vacations are torture for many people because when the rush to meet impossible schedules is over, they show no creativity in thinking of someting different and original to do. It's often easier to get back in the routine of work; but that doesn't provide a wholesome balance for their lives.

Don and I went to visit a minister and his wife one Monday. This pastor was so delighted that someone had livened up his day off. He said, "I can't get my wife to do anything different. She doesn't want a day off, so we just work around the clock." He died with cancer a year after that, and I remembered his pathetic look when he had said, "I wish we could go somewhere or do something different on Mondays."

There is really no right answer for controlling time. One man's requirement may totally conflict with anothers. But, leave room for your individual spontaneity. Work while you work and play while you play.

Our son is a great outdoorsman. There's very little he doesn't enjoy in hardy outdoor activity. He swims, skis, hunts, fishes, plays tennis. Steve is almost "religious" about his outdoor activities. Now that Steve has his own real estate business, he's had to shift his play activities considerably. But, he has made his work a joy; and now, even work has relaxing rewards for him.

People who have a wholesome grasp of the use of their time have established priorities. They can say yes to the important, and no to lesser demands. Everyone wants some of your time. Maybe everyone in your household clamors for your attention. When you function in a certain role—husband, wife, mother or father, daughter or son—you sometimes have to do what others want; but not always. If you allow one person to dominate, or decide for you what you will do, you'll become passive and incapable of making decisions.

Our daughter Ann had enrolled in a college in Indiana where my husband and I had both graduated. One month before school opened, she came in and announced, "I'm not going to that college. I'm going to Azusa Pacific College in California."

I had taken off my control of her life many years before, and I was glad that she was able to make decisions and stand by them. This poise and self-reliance gave her much security and trust in her own decision.

It is always oppressive to allow any one person to dominate our time or decisions. Retain some decisiveness and sparkle of individuality which is uniquely you.

Do some things you want to do. Don't waste time saying, "If only I were younger . . . or richer . . . or smarter . . . or more successful." Decide this is the best day possible to live, and start living. Don't be afraid to live, make new starts, new decisions, and to do things differently.

Don't cling to the past or allow *others* to cling to your past. Sometimes it's not too refreshing to see college schoolmates. They judge us on the data of our past, and refuse to recognize the God who is *now* in our lives. Let the past go. Go on to new companions who can appreciate your dreams and goals today, for dwelling in the past is deadening.

Making bold decisions is an important part of

controlling your time. I went into a fabric store the other day to find material for chair cushions and a small ice cream table. When I first entered the store, I thought, "This is going to be easy!" However, the more I looked, the harder it got, and the more confused and undecided I became. I was embarrassed that I had spent 1½ hours when I could probably have been satisfied much earlier had I made a deliberate decision. My head was hurting and my self-image was sagging. Indecision is paralyzing. Make a decision, even if it's not perfect. It can be changed.

I can't say too much about goal-setting. My husband and I sit down periodically and rewrite our goals. Sometimes these goals change, so we allow ourselves this freedom, but many goals have been met. Many are forthcoming. This saves us a lot of wasted motion and lets us zero in on the essentials. We try to give ourselves to that which we do best, and delegate responsibilities to others who are capable of doing some duties better then we. It frees us for our priorities and gives others a ministry.

Stop for a moment. Are you redeeming your time? Do your moves count? Do you stay busy all the time and accomplish nothing? Can you say, "No" sometimes without guilt? Can you make *play* out of work? Are you setting goals and allowing them to be updated with growth and time?

Try redeeming your time, and get more mileage out of life.

26. NOBODY LOVES ME

Each year our church's Women's Retreat climaxes

with a Love Feast. All the seminars and messages prior to that time are fragments of the whole. Love is the total of all truth, for God is love.

As I prepared to chair the Love Feast, I was trying to think what I could do to obtain more love for the occasion. My first thought was to spend an hour in prayer, asking for love; but it seemed the answer came quickly and spontaneously back to me: "Just give love away."

So I did not go pray for an hour. I went to the opening session and made myself available to meet anyone needing personal prayer during the seminars. As they gathered together and each one shared human problems and needs,we prayed for them one by one. My heart was revitalized and I was fully charged for the closing hour of the Love Feast.

I really learned a new lesson from this experience. I can have my shelves stacked with books on how to love. I can understand all the theological implications of love, but love is only made real by living.

Questions concerning loving were brought up, later during the week of seminars. My husband responded, "You can't receive more love as a Christian." God is love and you have God. You don't receive more of God than you already have. You only *release* that which you have and become a flow for love in a vital human relationship. Just as you don't receive more salvation, you receive a person, Jesus Christ, who is salvation and your participation with Him becomes more real to you as He is given away to others.

Watchman Nee was asked by a lady to pray for her to have more love in an unloving situation. He said, "No, I will not." She was shocked and disappointed. He then added, "Why should I pray for you to have what you already have?" Appropriate Jesus Christ in you, who is always loving, and you will love.

We really complicate what God has tried to make simple for us. We are ever learning but so often miss coming to the truth because we think one more catchy quote or psychological gimmick will accomplish what is already done in us and only needs to be appropriated by faith and released.

I was pondering these ideas when our telephone rang. On the other end of the line, a lady shared that her home was full of unloving attitudes and friction. She had purposely tried to live a godly life and be a loving person and display self-control. But she said nothing was working. In a fit of frustration, she had lashed out at her husband for his unlovely attitude. Then the Holy Spirit revealed to her that her perfectionist attitude had turned to judgment of others in her home. She had found that love was not a package all neatly wrapped and deposited in her heart so as to make her ethereal to others in the family. Love needed expression; yet her expressions of love had been withheld, waiting for others to come to that perfect level of performance. When that hadn't happened, the "mote in the eye" became a "beam." But when she realized the truth in the situation, she was freed to release others—in their temperaments and separate acts—and was able to freely respond to family members with unrestrained love.

On many occasions, misunderstanding can be chalked up to ignorance. When someone's behavior is bad, if we can retain this thought upper most in our minds, it somehow seems to soften the blow. Jesus even

demonstrated this on the cross when He said, "Father, forgive these people for they don't know what they are doing" (Luke 23:34).

Sometimes we are caught in the middle of a clash of opinions. There seems to be no common ground for the people involved because each person believes he is absolutely right and the other wrong.

If we could slip into the other person's shoes, and try to see a situation as he is seeing it, the walls could be less thick. As long as we cling to our absolute correctness and another's incorrectness, we have closed the door to all fellowship. In such a case we can praise the Lord that He is working in each life, and pray that God will reveal Himself in these circumstances. It takes much longer when we refuse to give a little, but sooner or later life will make us bend the knee to love or break ourselves. We can't invalidate the law and survive.

Some of the things which cause us prolonged pain are none of our business! We have meddled in another's life or affairs and, because we can't bend them to conform to our expectations, we shut them out with indifference. Sometimes saying, "So what . . . ?" we get freed of resentment. But if we only flip those words off the tongue and close our heart to all acceptance, we have really not solved our problem.

When Peter wanted to know how John would die, Jesus answered: "What is that to you? You follow me" (John 21:22). In other words, "Peter, it is none of your business about John." There is not blind indifference, but *before* we try to correct our outer world or even understand it, we need to consciously establish our hearts on the fixed principles that, "All is well," and that God works "out there" as well as "in here," without our own hearts and minds. It is surprising how often "out there" gets taken care of, or passes from our preoccupation. Two wrongs, won't make a right. Stop resisting and start loving.

You've probably had the experience of heading for a parking place right in front of the store where you were going to shop. However, someone else was as determined to get the spot as you. They drove right into the parking place behind you as you pulled ahead to allow the car who was leaving to back up. We can either conclude that the other driver was bad and acted like an "animal," or we can say, "Maybe he didn't see me." Perhaps we can step into his shoes and say, "He must feel badly today, I hope his day isn't ruined."

On our last trip to Hawaii, my husband had left a nice pair of cuff links on the dresser when we left our room. We didn't discover they were missing until we got home and he was dressing for Sunday morning church. The cuff links had been a gift from a friend, and each time Don wore them he prayed that God would work in the life of his friend. I knew losing the cuff links meant more than their tangible worth. As he silently went on dressing, I finally heard him conclude, "I'll just give those cuff links to whoever, Lord. Bless him and don't hold this against him." In that moment, the flow of life was unobstructed and love had made Don ready to be a channel for Divine current that morning. When we become disturbed, it's because we are "disturbable."

One of the hardest things to admit is that there is a possibility that we attract many disturbances to us. If we run into the same situation repeatedly, perhaps there is something within us which magnetizes it. Shakespeare said, "The world is full of griefs and graves, who knows but that the darkness is in man?" Certainly fostering loving relationships is not always easy, but who ever said "overcoming" life's obstacles would be easy? Praying for those persons who spitefully use you involves changing your thought toward them. It takes time, surrender and release. Snap the cord of resistance, and let the living waters gush from you. In that instant the divine awareness takes over and you are a lover. How do you get love? Give it away!

27. EXCELLENCE IS EXCITING

"Dear God,
Forgive me for flubbing the organ solo. I presumed too much when I thought I had memorized it. I want to do things perfect for you. It won't make any difference to you 100 years from now, will it, Lord?"

"I forgive you, little Ruth Ann. You're O.K. You are released."

"I'll just prepare my organ solos in advance from now on, Lord, Amen."

It was Palm Sunday morning. I had gotten all my cues and modulations from our new music director. I wanted to perform just right at the organ for God and for our new minister of music, for he too loves excellence. I had thought of everything but preparing an offertory number. When it was time for the offering I thought,

"Oh, this is Palm Sunday. I should play the 'Palms.'" I had played it many years from memory and presumptuously I started the refrain, "Open the Gates of the Temple." Then my mind froze and my fingers froze with it! I rushed to a familiar part of the song and found myself in a totally unfamiliar key.

I winced for all the music lovers in the choir and the congregation. Our music minister kept his face straight ahead; and my husband, waiting to preach, kept his head bowed in deep prayer. My fingers wandered for that lost chord (which will probably be found only in heaven).

At the conclusion of the offertory I was filled with embarrassment, so I hurriedly took my seat and wrote to God. If I didn't get rid of my problem quickly, I knew I would carry this condemnation for days.

Once I told God I was sorry, I felt better. I also forgave and accepted myself. I wrote a note to the music pastor to tell him I was sorry to make his program less than perfect. Once restored, I put the unfortunate incident all behind me and thought about next week's offertory.

I thought of the first two brothers who brought their own version of sacrifice to the Lord. One brother brought his own labors from the field. Abel brought the sacrifice of a lamb from the best of his flock. God had not asked for any sacrifice. Cain was refused by God because he did not bring the best to the Lord.

The world is made up of people who put out their versions of sacrifice. Some strive for excellence; to others it really doesn't matter. I believe in excellence. I love to watch the half-time activities at a college football game. The band, the majorettes, and the director move with precision. It's all so coordinated and perfect. I always think, "That's the way God's work should be, excellent! That's the way each life should be, excellent."

David said he would not offer to the Lord that which cost him nothing.

How you serve your family, your boss, your church, is an indication of your sacrifice. How you plan your meals, take care of your home, plan your day is your version of sacrifice.

The Bible tell us to do everything, "heartily as to the Lord" (see Colossians 3:23, *KJV*). "Heartily" means with enthusiasm. A person who cheerfully does more than he's required in his job soon has a better job. Life gives abundantly to him.

A brand new Christian gal who works in a large office shared a little bit about her past with me. Before her conversion, she stretched her coffee breaks, checked out early, and generally found ways to get something for nothing with the rest of the employees. Now that she has found Christ, her incentives have changed. She respects herself and loves to work. She does more than is required of her, and is even finding that her enthusiasm presents a threat to others who find all the ways to dodge work. Her employers are aware of her excellent work and she is enjoying promotions. She's "winning" by making an excellent sacrifice.

We have a wonderful Christian education director at our church. If someone gets discouraged with their responsibility, or feels taken advantage of, she says, "Oh, I'll do that!" Then she'll add the task to her other responsibilities until someone else joyously picks up that responsibility and releases her from it. She is giving an excellent sacrifice. Her creativity is growing and her organizational ability is expanding.

Luke 16:10 states, "He who is faithful in a very little thing is faithful also in much" (*NASB*).

My husband and I have made that Scripture the rule of our life. Be faithful when there's no one to see. Pick up the scrap of paper on the floor. Do the menial jobs. Sweep the floors. Do your alms in secret.

One of our friends had hired two boys to help them in their business. Boy Number I had been with them for a number of years. Boy Number II had worked for them only a few months. Boy Number II began to complain to Boy Number I that they weren't being treated fairly. A tense atmosphere was created between all of the people involved, so that working in close quarters was unbearable. It soon became necessary to dismiss Boy Number II, who then sought to get even. Boy Number I was mentally poisoned, and he too had to be dismissed. The day Boy Number I left, our friends showed them their will—in which they had purposed to leave their sizeable business to the two employees. These boys had lost by ceasing to give an excellent sacrifice.

Milton said, "There is not one last good." Serve in an excellent way. If you serve excellently, you will be rewarded openly.

28. KEEPING UP WITH THE JONESES

Our son, Steve, took us out for lunch the other day.

As we waited for our meal to arrive, we were discussing how painful it is to fall into the snare of attempting to keep up with someone else. In the course of our conversation, Steve made a statement which was a perfect commentary on the subject. He said, "Do you know who the Joneses are. It's me—last year." What a piece of wisdom! If we must compare, let us compete with what we were last year at this time.

God has made each of us unique. When any of us fall into the snare of trying to be a carbon copy of someone else we have forfeited our liberty and come under the hypnotic spell of another. This is particularly true in the world of things. To be caught in the social snare which strives to merit acceptance by the house we live in, the car we drive, the latest fad, the company we keep is truly a form of bondage.

These comparisons often plague the religious world. If we say it, do it, or act like a certain group, we hope to be accepted.

A man can be so much in God that he builds his own world. He doesn't need another man's foundation to hold him up. A man who isn't at his Source must run to this or that meeting, ever seeking to explode his spiritual faculties without any practical use to the world around him. He goes from "spiritual kick" to "spiritual kick." He leeches on his own kind, but harbors contempt for any other ideas, concluding them inferior to his own.

The man who is really in tune with God can possess an impartial love for all. He has no picks, no favorites. He gleans truth where it seems most unlikely because all of life teaches him. The Spirit of Truth is in him. He can take an active part in the affairs of the world without getting dirt on his soul. He is no isolationist. He is at home wherever he is. He sees the truth that lies behind appearances.

The man who competes with the Joneses of this life courts a monster. He is never at rest. He never comes to his own closet and shuts the door. He's never really sure of himself nor his God until he can again open the door (if he ever succeeds in closing it), and shares his love, his life, and himself with the world outside.

Such a completed person doesn't have to cut down his neighbor to elevate himself. He doesn't have to judge his neighbor's spiritual temperature to prove his superiority.

The man who competes is the man who is afraid to compliment. He is afraid that in so doing the favored one might grow better, feel better, be better. In doing so, the other person may outshine him. Consequently, he withholds approval. He will say, "I love you;" but never, "You did well." He will say, "I am praying for you;" but never, "Your life is blessing many."

The man who competes with the Joneses of this life "It's good for me but not for you." He lets "he be he" and "me be me." He doesn't crush another person's hopes nor pour water on his wildest dreams. He looks upon every broadening thought with child-like wonder, knowing that with every dreamer it is God acting like Himself. He chuckles in sincere delight that God would manifest Himself in another person. He knows that in God you cannot hope too much or dare too much. He delights to see growth, whether it's in someone else or in himself.

The man who ceases to compete measures another human being by what he is and not what he has. Such a man is not threatened by the genius of his employee. He seeks not to keep him poor, nor submerge his awakening abilities. He doesn't recruit for the selfish use of another's gifts or talents, but he recruits to make the other person richer, wiser, holier. If the other guy outruns him, he rejoices that like Barnabas, he has found a Paul and the world will be better for it. His riches consist in making others rich. He doesn't seek to be comforted, but to comfort. He doesn't seek sympathy, but to sympathize. He doesn't search for compliments, but to compliment. His life is a sacrament to others. He is happiest when he is pouring out his life, not pouring in. He sees the loner, the shy, the rejected, the torn, the confused. He sees in them potential healers which would be changed in a moment if they could unite with his God also.

Such a man is wiser than he knows. He accomplishes more than he thinks. He blesses without forethought. He gives without anxiety. He grows without effort. He loves without contemplation. He acts with spontaneity in a crisis. He becomes an immediate answer instead of a problem.

He has ceased his striving to outdo others. He only seeks to improve his own appropriation of the tools God has given him to succeed. If it is his best, he will not chafe when others appear more flamboyant than he. He knows he is one of a kind. He can do something better than anyone else. He knows that something is important to the world. Doing what he realizes he can do best, he knows he'll leave the world a better place and he will wear a crown.

Yes, *he* is the Joneses. He is the Mr. Jones of last year.

He is grander, more noble, than the Mr. Jones of last year. He is not at all content because he knows that at a future date he must—and he will—outrank the Mr. Jones of this year.

29. "THE PRINCIPLE OF PRAISE"

Many books are written today on the power of praise and thousands of people are finding peace, healing, and victory in life's situations.

Sometimes we wait for some special ingredient before we believe we have faith for something. The truth is that, "praise is faith at work." Praising can still the enemy.

What makes the difference between one Christian and another? The element of praise. Many times we find our needs are met—not when we're asking for them, nor when we are preoccupied with the need, but—when we praise God.

God is to be praised, adored, worshipped. When some of the super-pious Pharisees tried to stop the disciples from praising Jesus as He entered Jerusalem, Jesus rebuked them and said, "If they didn't cry out in praise, the rocks would" (see Luke 19:40).

Praise is not always easy. Sometimes the Bible says it's a sacrifice to praise.

Mrs. Freeborn's husband was a college pastor who lingered at the point of death from a heart attack. God spoke to Mrs. Freeborn from the Scriptures and said, "In everything give thanks."

"Lord, how can I possibly thank you that my husband is at the point of death?" Mrs. Freeborn asked.

"In everything give thanks, my dear," the Lord replied. Mrs. Freeborn began to praise. In a matter of hours, her husband responded and lived to declare the works of the Lord.

The secret of healing is often to praise and give thanks for the healing, right in the face of illness, before there is anything apparent for which to give thanks.

Why is praise so powerful? Because what you praise you *increase*. Praise liberates the life force that is pent up in you. It's like tapping a reservoir of energy.

People have praised themselves from weakness to strength, ignorance to intelligence, poverty to plenty, sickness to health. This is because praise brings us up to the *peak* of performance in body, soul, and spirit.

During a time of severe fatigue, the Lord really spoke to me, from Joel 3:10: "Let the weak say, I am strong" [*KJV*]. As I continually affirmed that verse, my body soon responded to my affirmation and I was alert with life once more.

Many people, including Christians, are chronic grumblers. They infect the whole atmosphere around them with faultfinding and complaining. I have seen people who have been liberated to a life of praise, and their entire families were transformed and converted.

Never yield to condemnation. Romans 12:14 says, "Bless . . . and curse not" (*KJV*). Condemnation rebounds to its sender, and what we condemn multiplies upon us. Some have said a description of evil repeated often intensifies the evil. That's why Paul said, "Fix your thoughts on what is true and good and right. Think about things that are pure and lovely, and dwell on the fine, good things in others. Think about all you can praise God for and be glad about" (Phil. 4:8). What the heart thinks, the mouth will eventually speak. The "inmost" becomes the "outmost."

Jesus said we were only to speak those things in church which edify. Perhaps that's why he said our conversation should be, "'Yes, yes' or 'No, no'; and anything beyond these is of evil" (Matt. 5:37, *NASB*).

A frustrated woman had become a mental and physical wreck through dwelling upon her problems. As she rehearsed her aches and pains, they grew worse. She proved that what you give attention to increases.

One day a counselor, after hearing her tales of woe, said, "Now that you've told me all that's wrong with you, tell me something that is right with you." She became angry and said, "There's nothing right with my health."

The counselor persisted, "There must be. You are able to walk, talk, hear, smell, taste, see. You are not bedridden nor helpless. If you did not have some degree of health, you'd be dead, and you *were able* to walk through that door."

The disgruntled lady finally agreed her little finger worked well; and she agreed, for one week, to thank God for her perfect little finger, for its life and wholeness.

After a few days she reluctantly admitted her health

was improving. In fact, her whole right hand could move without pain. She began a daily therapy of praise which returned her to a condition of much improved health.

When you are tempted to recite your ills, start praising God for the health you do have and thank God for increasing it.

Paul in his Epistles indicates that praise neutralizes stress. Faultfinding and critical, complaining words hasten a troubled situation.

If you're a chronic complainer, start doing just the opposite. Begin to praise everything and everybody.

Nehemiah said, "The joy of the Lord is your strength" (Neh. 8:10, *KJV*). Often, singing can break loose a dam of depression which has built up in our minds. We congest the nerves and important functions of our body when we're continually in a depressed state.

Laughter often shatters fear and increases hopefulness. Solomon says, in Proverbs 17:22, "A cheerful heart does good like medicine."

As a youngster growing up, I spent hours at the piano working out my moods. I often turned out the lights and just let my fingers flow over the keys, and very often I got up from the piano bench freed from my heaviness.

Force yourself to speak positive words of joy. Read psalms of praise *out loud*, sing joyous songs. Sing a repetitious song of happy affirmative words. Joy is one of nature's greatest medicines. Joy is always healthy. Some say the healthiest people are those who do not take events or themselves too seriously.

Sometimes problems arise out of a lack of gratitude, as Romans 1:28 tells us: ". . . when they gave God up and would not even acknowledge him, God gave them to doing everything their evil minds could think of." You can't be grateful and resent at the same time. Deuteronomy 28:45 states: "All these curses shall pursue and overtake you until you are destroyed—all because you refuse to listen to the Lord your God."

Jehoshaphat appointed singers to go before his soldiers chanting songs of praise and thanksgiving. David said, in Psalm 119:164, "I will praise you seven times a day because of your wonderful laws."

Let's get on with praise!

Prayer:

"We praise you today, dear Father, for all that you are to us. We praise you and thank you, in Jesus' name. Amen."

30. PRAISE WILL CHANGE YOUR LIFE

In the previous chapter, I shared what I've called the "principle of praise." Now I would like to consider some other facets of this vital, activating power—*Praise*.

Praise and thanksgiving activate the cells of our body. This charges the atmosphere around us. It releases increased amounts of energy and helps restore harmony to almost any situation.

Anna McGhie prayed for her brother for thirty years before she saw any visible sign of his conversion. She said that for thirty years she had praised God as though it were already an accomplished fact. It wasn't until the end of that 30-year-span that her brother came to her and asked the secret of her life. And it certainly didn't take her long to tell him! Someone asked Anna if she wasn't terribly overwhelmed, after praying for so long. Her wise reply was: "No, I was as happy thirty years ago as I am now, for through praise and faith I enjoyed his conversion before it ever came about."

If we want to *see* before we praise, we will probably never see nor praise. Don't wait for ideal circumstances to praise. There is always something good you can praise. As you do, your own good multiplies.

A child brought a stray dog to his mother, trying to convince her what a fine dog it was so she would allow him to keep the dog. The mother was totally unimpressed. Finally the boy said, "But Mom, look how nice he can wag his tail."

We usually never change anyone by a direct approach. "You ought to be better," seldom ever changes anyone.

I know mothers who pray beside their sleeping child. They pray affirmative prayers of blessing and declare these prayers do much more good than pleading with the child or even pleading with God.

Some folks always seem to have financial problems. There could be several reasons. Perhaps they've neglected the law of giving and receiving. The hole we give through is the hole we receive through.

It may be we are trying to live way beyond our financial means and have a spending spirit that is undisciplined.

Our financial problems can occur because we have become ungrateful and cynical. An ungrateful, cyncial attitude tends to empty our pocketbooks. There is an old proverb, "The ungrateful never escape."

The Bible says, in Proverbs 11:25, "The liberal man shall be rich! By watering others, he waters himself." Liberality, of course, means giving to others, not only of monetary things but of yourself, your smile, your appreciation, your time, your compliments or praise.

You may know the "law of affirming plenty" in your life and find out it's not working. If so, it may be because you're condemning your inability to pay your bills. You are cynical and critical when a bill arrives in the mail. You can even condemn your source of supply, or employer, and the inadequacy or insufficiency to meet your needs. Have you ever considered that money is the way God keeps the needs of His world supplied? Money feeds the mailman, the doctor, the milkman. Paul puts it so beautifully, in his letter to the Roman church, when he writes: "Pay all your debts except the debt of love for others—never finish paying that!" (Rom. 13:8). Pay your bills with gladness, knowing you are circulating the means to meet the needs of humanity to be fed, warned, and made glad.

As I mentioned in the previous chapter, we are to "bless . . . and curse not" (Rom. 12:14). Bless your creditors, bless your government. Be glad when you can tip a waitress and make her feel good for the day. God loves cheerful givers, happy givers, praising givers.

Recognition is a form of praise. Don't be afraid to recognize or affirm another person. Instead of demonstrating over your child's report card, tell him how his penmanship is improving. Description is a form of praise. To describe and dwell upon what you do not like, magnifies its importance and gives it negative power.

People who hate their job do a *poor* job, and are soon out of work. People who love their work, on the other hand, usually do a good job and are continually advanced. To say, "I hate my job," is a form of cursing; so don't be surprised if you soon don't have a job to hate. The Bible is emphatic: "Bless . . . and curse not." Circumstances don't always immediately change when you start to praise, but *you* will change. When you've become a miracle of praise, you send out a radiation of praise which is followed successively by a changed environment.

A dear friend was going through a traumatic problem with her husband's divided loyalties of love. In spite of the emotional pain, this friend continued to praise God. In fact, she increased her praise. The battle wasn't won in a day, but praise eventually rendered a victorious result. Her home was healed and her husband's love restored.

You can neutralize the effects of severe problems in your life right now with the cure of praise. Dare to praise God for a drunken husband. Dare to praise him for the good you see in his life. The obvious faults have blinded you to all of his virtues. Look! They're there! Begin to praise him.

Praise the child who frequently does all the things that irk you—on purpose. You'll confuse the pattern and remove the challenge of upsetting Mom and Dad.

Praise the pastor for his sermon you formerly said was dull. You'll be surprised how good it will sound next Sunday.

Praise the clerk for her smile, the mailman for keeping on the road in cold weather.

Smile at the person who takes "your" parking place just as you were going to park.

Praise your peer for some accomplishment, a job well done.

Praise the soloist, the custodian, the treasurer, the angry or hurt child.

You can turn someone else's world, as well as your own, into a paradise by the miracle of praise.

NOTES